DIPLOMACY

DIPLOMACY
Initiatives and Responses

Om Gupta

Publications

KALPAZ PUBLICATIONS

DELHI-110052

Diplomacy
Initiatives and Responses

Rs. 625

ISBN: 81-7835-326-1

Published in 2005 in India by
Kalpaz Publications,
C-30, Satyawati Nagar, Delhi-110052
E-mail : Kalpaz@hotmail.com

Laser Typesetting at : Shiva Infosystem, Delhi
Printed at : Salasar Imaging System, Delhi

Contents

Preface

At any given point of time, New Delhi is taking a diplomatic initiative through an aid project, high level visit, seminar, exhibition, sports event or even a statement. Almost at the same time one of the 120 odd countries that have their diplomatic missions in Indian capital is responding either to an earlier initiative or a proposed move. These initiatives and responses make New Delhi a most happening place in the global diplomacy, both at a bilateral and multilateral levels. This book deals with numerous case studies pertaining to the period 1992-97. In fact it is not a structured book in the classical mould. It is a collection of weekly columns that appeared in mid-day under the two slots Diplomacy and Demarche courtesy the then editor John Dayal for which I shall always remain indebted to him. Though mid-day is an afternoon paper meant for leisure reading still the column was widely read in the diplomatic circles and it had given me an easy access to the missions and South Block.

The column originate from the need of reporting on these silent and generally unsung moves and countermoves by India and the rest of the world. There is no single department or ministry of the government of India that doesn't contribute to diplomacy. But it is taken as a routine matter and nobody talks about it except the concerned people. Not only this, most of the high profile visits except from the five permanent members of the

Security Council and of course Pakistan rarely find a mention in the national media. The concerned embassies do make some right kind of noises but the media tends to ignore it under the pretext that their readership is not interested. This book will place such visits and moves in the right context.

While writing this column I also came across several honorary consuls who are distinguished Indians appointed as honorary representatives of countries like Belize, Costa Rica etc. They do as much as regular missions do but they are considered to be outcastes both by South Block and the embassies. There is another gray area called UN missions who are doing a great job in the realms of global diplomacy but they also rarely get their due.

This book would not have seen the light of the day without the kind indulgence of the scores of joint secretaries of South Block and numerous ambassador friends especially the Latin American block that has been a subject of my journalistic and academic pursuit in the 1990s. I am grateful to them. Similarly my colleague at Rai University, Shikha Gupta went through the manuscript and gave it a definite shape.

Last but not least, I am indebted to my wife Arati Thapa who was also a fellow columnist in the same newspaper and an active participant in the buttonholed tete-a-tete during the numerous diplomatic parties in that period. We used to exchange notes and sift our relevant bits and pieces of inputs for our respective columns. What a hair splitting exercise used to be that week after week for five long years. I have failed in convincing her to come out with a collection of her columns that I am sure would be far more interesting as it dealt with the colourful cocktail circuit but her discretion has kept the readers away from that delight. I am sure one day she would change her mind and oblige her subjects and readers with those juicy details.

Om Gupta
New Delhi, August 2005

1
Diplomacy at Large

No Come, No Go — No Ine Seems to Bother About

Indian diplomacy being humbled in international fora while seeking a vote or support is familiar phenomena but, last fortnight it got a drubbing in entirely unexpected quarters. In a bizarre sequence, India wanted to extradite Ottavio Quattrocchi from Kuala Lumpur and Amir Bhai from Dubai and dispatch Charles Sobhraj to France. It did not succeed in any.

This is not the first time when the charges made by Indian investigative agencies have not been taken at face value. Some time back, the self-styled Khalistan leader J S Chauhan had taken refuge in Equador and when Indian government wanted him back for a trial, the host country didn't oblige.

Whatever may be the contention of CBI, the fact remains that the present political scenario in the country does not generate any confidence in the rest of the world about our intent and purpose.

Law and order apart, there is a diplomatic angle whenever we want a criminal back home or to be sent away. It so happened that foreign secretary Salman Haider was in Paris when the application for deporting Sobhraj was pending there. At the request of the Home Ministry, our foreign secretary did try to convince the French authorities, but according to reports, there have been no definite answers as the papers in France are crying foul on the bikini-killer about to be given a home in France.

It is sad commentary on diplomats and other image-builders that our credibility is so low. I met Sobhraj outside chief metropolitan magistrate Prem Kumar's court in Tees Hazari this week, forcing my way through a swarm of fellow reporters from the national and international television networks.

He looked more of a celebrity dressed in his now almost trademark golf cap, waistcoat and blue denims than a psychopath killer who played with the Indian judiciary for two decades to his advantage.

It is hard to believe how he could escape the almost certain gallows in Thailand and was allowed to be interviewed, filmed (and later escaped) to become a living legend, albeit an in-famous one. If India has treated him comfortably for so long, why do they want to dump him in France now. If he is a threat in India, is he not one in France too? If he is half French, is he not half Indian as well? Are Indian diplomats and the law enforcing agencies able to answer these ticklish questions?

Sobhraj and Quattrocchi hogged the limelight because of their high profiles. What about those hundreds of drug peddlers who go scot-free every year in different parts of the world because either there is no extradition treaty with many countries or there is lack of evidence. Why go far, even Nepal has become haven for anti-India activities, courtesy ISI of Pakistan and other anti-national elements. Even small time criminals from India take the first available means of transport to seek refuge in the outskirts of Kathmandu.

Diplomacy has its own limitations because of its subtle character. Law enforcing and expediting the restoration of order is not one of its primary functions. Refugees of the genuine and the not so genuine varieties seeking political asylum or taking advantage of legal lacunae have become the order of the day. Different kinds of skills are required to deal with these new situations. Since such matters are considered political in nature, the initiatives to resolve them should also come from quarters other than diplomatic.

Chanakyapuri-II in the making

It's been a hectic week as far as practicing diplomacy for the Indian government is concerned. South African President Nelson Mandela arrived to a rousing public reception and a gracious Mahaswheta Devi received the Jnanpith award from him. Talks between India and Kashmir reached its zenith at the Hyderabad house and finally the Sultan of Oman Qaboos Bin Syed has made his maiden visit to our country.

Although I am tempted to write about all these countries, I take a detour of my thoughts to a place nearer home since I have written about South Africa and Kashmir in my earlier columns. About Oman, perhaps in my next column!

This week for personal reasons. I was compelled to take a trip to Papankalan and Dwarka where I was told Delhi-ites were investing money in properties (read flats). Some of my friends who have forced their reluctant husbands to invest there couldn't stop telling about the place. I had to see the place! Here I found that it wasn't just the Delhiwallahs but the diplomatic community as well as who was making a beeline for it.

At last, the search for the second diplomatic enclave is over. Fifty years ago when India became an independent country, it generously offered barren land (read as the most prized land today) and named it Chanakyapuri for whichever country wanted a piece of land for a song albeit on a reciprocal basis. Countries such as China, the then Soviet Union and Britain managed to get whatever they cast their eyes on.

Most of the Asian and African countries were still under the yolk of foreign domination who taking a cue from India, intensified their respective freedom movements and became sovereign nations. India was the epitome of freedom, democracy and self-governance. Hence, setting up a diplomatic mission in New Delhi was a natural corollary. Soon Chanakyapuri fell short of accommodating all the new-nations. They sprawled all over the city first in adjoining areas including Vasant Vihar, West End, Anand Niketan and Shanti Niketan and then to other notable names such as Golf Links, Sunder Nagar, Jor Bagh and what have you. But for security and other reasons, the desire to huddle together and live with a community in a diplomatic enclave never diminished.

South Block took a plea that it was not its responsibility to provide accommodation to all and sundry, but the political masters kept the pressure on.

Eventually, places such as Vasant Kunj and Gurgaon were offered, but they fell through for various considerations.

Now comes the good news! A couple of kilometres behind the international airport is the scene of an unprecedented construction activity ever seen in the annals of the Capital's history.

A total area of 65 square kilometres was earmarked in early 1980s to fulfill the growing needs of the city's ever increasing housing demands. The area was known after the nucleus village called Pappankalan but rechristened as Dwarka, reminiscent of the mythological capital of Lord Krishna.

The journey to Dwarka from any other part of the town is an arduous and painstaking as must have been for the Yadavs in that age. Krishna wanted to have his capital in a haven so that the oft repeated onslaughts of the neighbouring kings be staved.

The concept behind Dwarka is to save prospective dwellers from enemies such as pollution, traffic and congestion.

Out of the total area, 20 square kilometres have been offered to diplomatic missions maintaining their chanceries and houses at exhorbitant rents in all parts of South Delhi. Many diplomats have found the place so interesting that they have already taken majestic farmhouses on Najafgarh-Gurgaon highway.

These farmhouses are inconspicuous in their exterior look but are fairy lands once you step in. In fact the tendency to hire out the fanciful farmhouses on the entire Mehrauli-Gurgaon road. Delhi-Jaipur highway and the adjoining hamlets have come handy to those owners who didn't know what to do with their properties after having built them.

Frankly speaking, Delhiwallas have proved to be copycats when it comes to farmhouses, but they have not learnt the art of living in style. At best, these archtype farmhouses are gaining dust in the absence of maintenance and frequent use. They do not make news when there is a raid on a Jain of hawala fame or when an investigative teams knocks the door of an erstwhile leader. There are occasional parties by the owner or his friend and at times it is loaned or rented for an evening. The desire of ambassadors and other senior diplomats to taste the fineries invested by the glitteratis have proved to many businessmen disguising as farmers sometimes do takeover.

The best example of this hypocrisy is the so-called Sainik Farms which also boasts of at least two ambassador residents. The idea behind offering land for farmhouses was to inculcate the traits of farming and gardening among the city dwellers but that seems to have fallen flat on its face and these places have become addresses of fun and frolic.

The prospective diplomatic enclave in Dwarka is a good news for embassies but bad for landlords, farmhouse owners and real estate business because the 5,000 odd ex-patriate community in Delhi has changed the economies of the landlord-tenant relationship. This is the best bet which any property owner can put his stakes on. Though it will take another decade before a full-fledged Chanakyapuri-II comes into being, but already the black money peddlers are making a bee-line around the Indira Gandhi international airport to claim their share in the latest pie.

Indian diplomacy at its best

Never before in the remit past an international conference involving 80 countries from six continents was organised with such perfection as the one recently held at Vigyan Bhawan.

The subject was also unprecidented; men, women partnership in politics.

The timing was perfect too: the Indian Parliament is seized with a bill to preserve a quota for 33 per cent women members and there could not have been a more befitting finale when the then Prime Minister H. D. Deve Gowda announced in a packed hall that he would see to the smooth passage of the bill in the Budget session starting today.

Not that the conference was devoid of non-issues that ranged from facility to speak Hindi and the demand to include Phoolan Devi in the Indian delegation.

Hindi was promptly added to the conference languages which includes English, French, Spanish, Chinese, Japanese and Russian. No one gave math importance to Phoolan Devi who seems to be playing with law once again. The ascendence of Phoolan Devi to the membership of the Indian Parliament from the ravines of Chambal showed the strength of Indian democracy and now Phoolan is being asked to appear before a court of law is the fair play of Indian tradition. However, that is a different issue altogether.

This conference debated at length on the vital issues like training women for politics, role of media in projecting women participation and last but not least how to increase women participation in the decision-making process of the country, it was unanimously felt that statutory and structural changes would not help.

The need was to have a change in the attitude which would do away with the gender bias.

During the five day conference Vigyan Bhawan was busy with a flurry of activities. Men and women from many continents and across many oceans were engaged in issues which are a concern of a nation and a family alike.

It was a lest of Indian hospitality as well, Ashoka Hotel the flagship of ITDC again came handy to accommodate the largest chunk of delegates as well to host large dinners on its front lawns and cultural exposition in its convention hall.

The conference witnessed a dismal indifference on the fart of Indian media, pointed out sadly by a Malaysian delegate.

The popular opinion of the delegates was that not many national dailies gave the conference the attention that it deserved.

The media centre seemed quite barred in the Vigyan Bhawan annexe.

However, Indian participation with the largest delegation of over a dozen members, headed by the veteran CPM parliamentarian Geeta Mukherjee who also pioneered the women reservation bill was more than satisfactory. But it was Najma Heptullah's show all the way, who had laboriously worked for this moment for almost two years.

The idea it seems began in the Beijing World conference three years ago. She had a willing Lok Sabha speaker P.A. Sangma who lent her guidance and support. It is difficult to understand what goes into organising such a mammoth conference which requires years of planning and preparation.

A lot of our South Asian friends from Singapore, Hong Kong and Bangkok boast of their conference facilities but participants of conferences like NAM, CHOGAM and G15 held in other parts of the world vouch that India is no less, if not better, India had its own surprises to offer and this became obvious when the participants went ga-ga over the February Sun shining outside and the serene twilight oozing out of the glass terrace.

Successful Performance from Diplomatic to Cricketing Field

Ever since South Africa opened its diplomatic mission in New Delhi, the relations between the two countries are quite naturally becoming better. South Africa has always maintained its special feeling for India because of Mahatma Gandhi who began his non-violent movement in South Africa. Therefore when South Africa's deputy president, Tbabo Mbeki declared, in a press conference at the Hyderabad House in New Delhi, that it was an emotional moment for all the South African delegates to be in India, one couldn't be surprised.

Thabo Mbeki is widely reported to be the next president of the African National Congress (ANC) after president Mandela. This might be after the 1997 organisational elections of ruling ANC and the subsequent general election some time later.

Thabo Mbeki was at his diplomatic best while parring questions from a select few Indian journalist. The questions were on important issues like Ghali's successor as UN Secretary General, South Africa's snapping of diplomatic relations with Taiwan, Morrocan support to ANC to ward off Sehrawi independence, India's permanent membership of Security Council, its refusal to sign CTBT and Johannesburg which could be the gateway between India and Latin America.

Understandably, the South African leader did not want to comment on any of these issues despite a very fruitful visit to improve bilateral relations. But then that is what the modern diplomacy is all about.

Lets leave the global issues for the right fora and talk business! On that score, four agreements were signed between the two countries, thus allaying Indian fears about its investment in South Africa.

A grand reception was hosted by the South African high commissioner, Jerry M. Matsila at the Sahajahan Hall at Taj Palace where I met an Indian member of the South African delegation, Ricky Naidoo. Tall and bespeckled, Naidoo had nothing Indian about him except his last name. "You are an Indian?" I asked. "I am a South African," he replied. "Really, you had no feeling when you landed in India era as an Indian." I prodded again. "It was like landing in any of the European countries," he replied. "But yes, if I were to land in Angola or Zimbabwe or Nigeria I would feel at home," he further added. As I mixed with other guests of the party, my thoughts went back to Naidoo again and again, wondering, did all Indians who settled abroad feel the same?

Now that is a very interesting dilemma. Over ten million people of Indian origin live across the globe. They include foreign citizens, Non-Resident Indians (NRI), work permit holders and those who went on a tourist visa and stayed back. For those Indians who adopted an alien land as their own and settle there, Nehru had said the last word about them, "If you adopt a new land, belong to it." But then he was a visionary, lesser mortals are not. How can you stop an Apache Indian visiting his *nani* in a dusty village of Punjab after more than two decades. Guyanese President Chedi Jagan recalling his village in Begu Sarai. Even Clinton evoked an emotional chord when he visited Ireland. Is it possible to delink yourself from your roots even if you transport them? Hats off to Naidoos of South Africa. That's the right thing to do, if you want to survive and progress in South Africa.

At the party I also met India's new suave foreign affairs spokesman, Tahmeez Ahmed who is likely to takeover from Arif S. Khan from the beginning of next year and his beautiful lawyer wife who undoubtedly will soon integrate into Delhi's elite circuit. Ahmed at present is the deputy chief of the mission in Pretoria where he was sent last year after a successful stint in London.

With Mbeki's visit and the grand finale to the three test series at Green Park (Kanpur), South Africa has rounded off its campaign of hitting sixes and fours launched earlier this year at Hyatt Regency by the high commissioner Malsila. Here is the score board. Unlike the South African cricket team who were restricted not only to fours but ones and twos by our cricketers, the high commissioner has been able to score sixes all the way with his sincere efforts.

It is undoubtedly a happy situation because the score board of bilateral relations between India and South Africa seems to be shining all the more. As Mbeki puts its, Gandhi and Nehru had laid a strong foundation for Indo-South African relations. It is incumbent on present generations to build a strong edifice for future.

At the moment, cricket seems to be the strongest binding force between the two countries. Indian cricket team has travelled a long distance since the legendary Nelson Mandela, president of South Africa invited the Indian cricketers at the request of the Indian South Africans. Hope Sachin Tendulkar and his boys would give an equally befitting performance when they visit South Africa later this year.

Changing Face of Latin American Diplomacy

Into-Latin American relations had suffered from distance, ignorance and indifference since independence. But not any more. The present lot of Latin American ambassadors, which incidentally includes five ladies, have made all the difference. Today, bilateral trade between India and the countries of that region has shown an upward swing. Former Indian President Shankar Dayal Sharma visited Trinidad and Tobago to attend the 150th anniversary of India's arrival at Trinidad and Tobago and the then prime minister Narasimha Rao visited Columbia and Argentina he same year to participate in NAM and G-15 summits respectively in the same year. This year Brazilian president, Cardoso was the chief guest at our Republic Day celebrations.

These bilateral visits at the highest level included the delegations of important businessmen which resulted in the agreements between Chambers of Commerce and the formation of Latin American division in India Trade Promotion Organisation (ITPO).

Argentina has been holding annual essay competitions to promote Indo-Argentina perspectives among students and Panama has announced an essay competition in the memory of one of its renowened poets, for whom India was a source of inspiration. A school in R K Puram has been named after the legendary revolutionary Jose Marti of Cuba. Incidentally there are already two roads named after Latin American heros Benito Juarez and Simone Bolivar.

Jawaharlal Nehru University has produced more than a dozen Ph.Ds and over forty M.Phils, in Latin American history, economy and diplomacy under the internationally renowned Latin Americanist R. Narayanan. Latin American division in Goa University is all set to repeat JNU's remarkable achievement. Last year a similar division was opened in Lucknow University. The Spanish and Portuguese language school at JNU has trained a generation of Spanish experts in Delhi who have made the travel and trade between India and Latin America in their lingua franca. There have been silent studies done by ICRIER, Germanic and Romance studies programme of Delhi University. Information and system for non-aligned and other developing countries have created a right kind of atmosphere to explore the possibilities of gainful exchanges in various fields.

The enterprising Indian businessmen from far flung areas like Ludhiana and Jalandhar to Jaipur and Ahmedabad have created markets for their cycles, engineering goods, pharmaceutical and gems. A special mention must be made of individual efforts of people like Pali Singh of Nancy Crafts and Vivek Aggarwal of United Wheels and TG Veeraprasad of Machines and Tools.

At the official level, the present finance minister PA Chidambaram should be credited for placing Indo-Latin American trade on the even table supported by the minister of state for external affairs Salman Khurshid who's still by missed the diplomatic community in Delhi. The Latin American division under the dynamic leadership ot three successive joint secretaries KM Meena (presently high commissioner in New Zealand), Ram Mohanji presently ambassador in Chile) and now Sanjay Singh have made substantial difference in India political and diplomatic perceptions towards the region.

No wonders that India has reopened its embassy in Colombia, set up a second mission in a Argentina and

Brazil, appointed honourable consuls in many countries of central America where we do not have full fledged missions. This has been reciprocated by Nicaragua, Grenada and Belize.

All this has been possible because of the present set of ambassadors who have created an awareness through food and cultural festivals, exhibitions, national day celebrations, newsletters and participation in various activities organised by Indians.

Their presence and interaction is marked by an air of informality and cordiality never seen before. Ambassadors like Carmenza Jaramillo of Colombia, Elda Sampierto, Olga Chamero Trials of Cuba and Joceylen Henriquez of Venezuela have successfully organised the trips of their ministers and their counterparts in each other's countries. They are accessible who have adapted themselves to the Indian cultural ambience and social milieu with an amazing ease. All of them are professional diplomats drawn from foreign services having served various international capitals. Indo-Latin relations are safe in their hands.

Solidarity in the Golden Year of Independence

Ever since Lalit Mansingh has taken over as secretary (West), the relations between India and Latin American countries are on an upward swing. A charming diplomat that he is, with a deep interest in arts and culture, the Latinos have responded with matching reciprocity. After the highly successful visit of president Fujimori of Peru, there is a distinct possibility of president Carlos Menem of Argentina visiting India to express solidarity with the commemoration of our 50th anniversary of Independence.

If he does that it will be his second visit in a short span of four years. Last time, he came to takeover the chairmanship of G-15 in the New Delhi summit.

Ambassador Alberto Louis Daverede was here this week for bilateral political consultations. He is equivalent to a secretary in Argentina foreign ministry. While talking to him at a luncheon hosted by Mansingh at the Jahanara banquet hall of hotel Taj Palace. I got a chance to update Indo-Argentina affairs.

According to ambassador Daverede, there is an immensely growing interest for two Indian things in Argentina textiles and yoga. Many 'Hindu' garment shops have come up in Buenos Aires which sell beautiful Indian fabrics and design. In fact, he himself had long shopping list given by his family to get the real stuff from Delhi.

The business card sent by Mansingh's office had an interesting portfolio added to Daverede's designation, under secretary for foreign policy in the ministry of external relations and worship. The guest explained that Roman Catholicism being the straight religion of his country, the then government some decades ago thought it imperative to safeguard the interests of other religions imported from different parts of the world. These included various denominations of Hinduism including yoga. Did he ever have to deal with a situation regarding Indian sects? The ambassador replied in affirmative and told that once some sort of an aberration in the form of sex and violence was brought to his notice by a small group but it was sorted out soon. Notwithstanding this isolated case Indian government, the living Sai Baba of Pullapurthy has attracted the veneration no less than president Menem and most of his cabinet. He had devoted full five minutes to this subject during his conversation with the then visiting Indian Prime Minister PV Narasimha Rao who had gone there to attend the G-15 summit in Buenos Aires in 1995. A bemused Indian leader could only mutter that now he had provided a helipad near Sai Baba's hermitage so that Argentina guests could fly directly to their adopted lord.

Incidentally, Sai Baba devotees form the largest incoming travellers from Argentina every year.

But the Indian response is not quite similar. In fact, fly-by-night business operators caused a big consternation amongst Latin American embassies in New Delhi when on an average the passports of about a dozen prospective travellers were presented for visa marking in almost every mission. It was Argentina which first discovered this and joined heads with other counterparts.

To their utter shock, they found that Latin American visas were being used to disembark at a convenient airport in Europe. When they asked the travel agents bringing the passports to produce the concerned visitors, they were horrified to know that the passport-holder neither knew English nor the destination. Or even when he intended to fly. The dubious travels were stopped on the tracks. Now visas are granted after a thorough personal interview.

But Indo-Argentine relations are not marred by such queer incidents. In fact, the bilateral relations between the two countries have grown by leaps and bounds ever since the present ambassador Elda B Sampeitro took over in March 1994. The essay competition on Argentina perspectives has entered the fifth year.

The unassuming newsletter produced by the mission is one of the best because of the immense information it gives about Argentina in particular and Latin America in general. There have been regular exchanges at the academic level. The scholarly interest to research on Argentina political history and economy is growing.

Argentina was the first country where India had set up its trade mission, way back in 1943. Since then, through various bilateral visits undertaken by President Zail Singh (1983), Vice President Sarvapalli Radhakrishnan (1954). Prime Minister Indira Gandhi

(1968) and Rao (1995), ministers Krishna Menon (1954), Pranab Mukherjee (1982) and recently Jai Narain Nishad.

These visits were primarily to explore trade and other ties. Argentines reciprocated these gestures by the visits of president Arturo Frondizi and Menem (1994), governors of Cordoba, and Negro Eduardo Angelos and Horatio, Messacessi and minister Felix Alberto (1982).

Argentines have helped twice, once in 1946 and later in early 1980s through shiploads of grain in our moment of crisis. There is a large settlement of Sikh farmers and traders in the north Argentina town of Salta. President Zail Singh went out of his way to meet these Argentine Sikhs during his visit in 1983. President Menem had proposed during his visit in 1994 that some Indian farmers should migrate to cultivate in the barren lands of his country. The proposal is still pending.

On the cultural front, the bilateral ties go still far back in this century. The accidental stop-over of our Nobel laureate Rabindra Nath Tagore in Argentina because of sudden indisposition on his way to Lima, Peru turned out to be historical milestone, courtesy his hostess Victoria Ocampo who continues to be a subject matter of literateurs in both countries.

Now her inheritor Rene Cura continues to carry forward the legacy through a journal called Indisa and a centre Anand Bhawan in Buenos Aires. These efforts are supplemented by Swami Shivananda's Yoga Ashram and that of Brahmakumaris which attract a lot of local people.

Finally, the trade relations are looking up with the establishment of an assembly unit of Hero Motors. Until recently, Tata trucks were quite popular, but now are facing tough competition from Mercedes, I agree with ambassador Sumpteiro that Indian companies should think about setting up local assembly units if they want to compete globally. Mere trading won't help for long.

However, Mahindra jeeps continue to be immensely popular.

Evolve Diplomacy to Fetch Global Business

The national day celebration of the tiny English speaking Central American country of Belize once again brought into focus the role and the need of honorary consuls in the world of diplomacy. Arithmetically speaking, India has full-fledged embassy level relationship with 100-odd countries on either side, that is their missions here and ours abroad. But India enjoys diplomatic relations with almost 200 countries out of the count of 241, the remainder is handled either through concurrent accredition by an ambassador posted in a relatively more important neighbourly country. That is not the best way to deal with the small but sovereign nations who enjoy equal vote at international fora such as the UN (which we need desperately more often than not on issues including Kashmir) and rights when it comes to dealing with other countries. For example, our high commissioners in Australia and New Zealand are also Indian envoys to other Polynesian islands in South Pacific. But many a times Indian high commissioners are not able to visit these independent nations to present their credentials. There cannot be bigger insult to a friendly country that you announce the appointment of an ambassador and he does not offer the minimum courtesy of introducing himself to the concerned head of state. This problem can be easily solved by the appointment of honorary consuls. That is appointing a local citizen of that country with whom you want to have regular diplomatic relations to promote trade and other ties. There are many such countries who have appointed Indian businessmen such as Mohinder Singh Salmi to represent our country in Belize consulate. One of the main functions of these consuls, as the title suggests, is consular service that is to issue visas. Such appointments are made on the basis of the credibility and the status the businessman employs in Indian economic and political circles. Visa apart, the consuls also expediate the potential of the business between his own country and the nation he represents. Sahni distributed a very useful investment guide for Belize at the reception hosted at Kamal Mahal in Maurya Sheraton. This investment guide can inspire any enterprising Indian businessman to chip in his money in the flourishing economy of a country where many Indians have turned their fortunes since many decades. The reception was attended" by the diplomats of almost every country which has a mission here. Some of them such as Trinidad and Tobago and Myanmar were present at the ambassadorial level and also the honorary consuls of Nauru and Costa Rica which speaks volumes about the popularity Sahni enjoys.

He had also invited scores of Indian businessmen who came accompanied with their wives decked in pearls, diamonds and flashing chiffons and silks, so that they could interact with the commercial counsellors and other functionaries of the foreign mission here. The reception was devoid of the formal veneer which engulfs such celebrations. There was an atmosphere of informality and bonhomies. Sahnis were taking particular care to make every guest comfortable and unlike most of such does the guests.

But there was a conspicuous absence of the Ministry of External Affairs on this occasion. Unfortunately, South Block does not give the due importance to these honorary consuls. This subject calls for a review at the highest political level. As mentioned above, in the absence of full ambassadorial representation honorary consuls are the best bet for diplomatic initiatives. They are appointed at the recommendation of the concerned foreign government and after the concurrent approval of MEA, they enjoy the trust of the both. Being drawn from public life and generally the corporate sector, their fundamentals are clear on how to promote business since it is business that is paramount in diplomacy these days. Not being a part of the establishment they are free to take decisions in the interest of both the countries. They are hand-picked for the acumen they possess with a specifically brief assignment. That is not the case with the serving officers of the foreign service who are governed by an elaborate procedural rigmarole for historical reasons the continuity of region and the interest of the diplomat is overlooked while being appointed eg. a European expert could be sent to Africa and vice versa. That is not the case with honorary consuls. Kartar Singh Bhalla has been representing Nauru since 1985 and has accomplished his job with impeccable record. It is high time honorary consuls are upgraded in Indian diplomatic perceptions.

2
State Visits : Goodwill Missions

Kant's Visit to Brazil

New dimension to bilateral ties

The Institution of the Vice-President of India is the most functional epitome of the federal structure of the country. Being the ex-officio chairman of the upper house of Indian Parliament, he not only represents but is the custodian of the hopes and aspirations of the constituent states. Today, when the centre-state relations are once again under severe stress and strain, the sane counselling by the second seniormost citizen of the country can be of great value. Since six out of ten have graduated to the presidency, it can easily be inferred that there is not much of a difference between the caliber and competence of the incumbents. And if some were not offered the highest constitutional position there must have been some considerations other than their ability and acumen. No wonder the Vice-Presidents are also invited and requested to represent the countries at international and multilateral fora where for some other pressing engagements the Prime Minister is unable to go. It happened in the case of the last G-15 summit when the present Vice-President Krishan Kant, led the Indian delegation.

Similarly, the Vice-Presidents are also invited in their official capacity by their counterparts from different parts of the world. Shri Krishan Kant paid an official visit to Brazil in October 2000. It was his second high profile interaction with a Latin American country. In 1999 he was the host to the visiting Uruguayan Vice-President. At the G-15 summit also, he had an occasion to meet the leaders of the seven Latin American countries Argentina, Brazil, Jamaica, Mexico, Venezuela. When a senior leader like the Vice-President represents his country, he is treated like a statesman because he is not governed by the mundane day to day diplomacy and businesslike approach. He is heard and discussed for the vision and perspective he has acquired in the long innings he has played in his public life. Because of his daily exposure in the vibrant parliamentary procedures and discussions, courtesy being the presiding officer of the senior house of the national legislature, he has an additional advantage of past and present. The mandarins of South Block may hold any opinion about the utility of the foreign visits of the President and Vice-Presidents of India but having been a member of many such trips. I can vouch that the instant rapport which these constitutional institutions form, the active politicians fail to achieve because of their pragmatic approach.

India, at least in Latin America is still considered to be a land of ancient wisdom, spiritualism and moral values rather than technical and economic advancement. This is reflected in the planeloads of Latins arriving at the ashrams of Satya Sai Baba and various other ashrams in different parts of the country. During my many visits, of that part of the world, I didn't see any major city without a yoga centre. They still look upto us whenever they want a break from their materialistic life. Therefore when senior statesman like leader visits their country the curiosity to reach out to him is write large on their faces. Because of this single factor each visit by at the higher level is worth many such diplomatic visits made by routine politicians. As far as Brazil is concerned there are many similarities and commonalities to draw from each other's experience in the fields of agriculture, poverty alleviation, environment and health. Recently the health minister and the deputy chairman of the Brazilian parliament visited Delhi. During conversations with them, it was revealed that they are very keen to learn from our land reform experiment and child health care programmes.

Indo-Brazilian ties in particular and Indo-Latin American relations in general have not progressed the way we would have liked them to. In my opinion, the only reason is our traditional approach towards cultivating them. These countries are different because of the cultural, linguistic and other reasons like distance and consequent mindsets. They should have been approached and dealt differently. One such approach is the visits by senior statesmen like the one of Vice-President Krishan Kant.

Indian NAM Camaraderie with Yugoslavia

Yugoslavia is one of the most unfortunate countries of our times. Almost overnight it got disintegrated into four parts and continues to bleed for ethnic and racial reasons. It is one of those countries which has been closest to India on account of the principle of non-alignment propounded by three great personalities, Nehru, Nasser and Tito.

In Delhi one of the main roads is named after Joseph Broz Tito, even though more than half of the world does not recognise the separate nomenclature of the erstwhile Yugoslavia because they think it should be known as Serbia because of whom, the other three states walked away from the confederation. But India still gives proper regard to its NAM co-founder, which was evident from the presence of Vice-President Krishan Kant and his wife at the constitution day vin d' honneur celebrations organised in the enclosure of chancery on Shantipath in April 1998.

I think such celebrations are rare in this building which now seems to bear a haunted look. A lone man India's NAM camraderie with Yugoslavia guards the somewhat decaying entrance of the embassy.

Though on this occasion, as expected, the security seemed unending. This mind boggling security was a sad reminder of the bloody clashes still taking place in Bosnia-Herzegovina for a separate Muslim nation. However, a large number of guests comprising diplomats, journalists and businessmen were present on this occasion to express their solidarity with Yugoslavia and to talk about business, politics and globalisation. Inside the building the walls are still adorned with the pictures of Rajendra Prasad, Radhakrishnan, Jawaharlal Nehru and Mahatma Gandhi.

The other nations, which separated from the Yugoslavia, such as Croatia and Montenegro were conspicuous by their absence, reminding one of similar boycotts by the two Koreas of each other, of the Arab nations by the Israel and vice versa.

It is only India and Pakistan that continue to grace each other's celebrations, invite celebrities and exchange dialogues whenever the heat gets too much. Even though expelling each other's diplomats for the pettiest of reasons, has become the most common expression of anger between the two countries.

This week Delhites saw the launch of Levis, America's dream jeans out to globalise—call it Americanisation of the Indian market, if you so wish. Even if the fabric is imported from India itself to be stuck, designer labelled and sent back to India.

Ghungroos at Maurya Sheraton bubbled with chilled bear, resonant voice of Sunny Sarid and sexy twenty–somethings, who dressed up for the occasion and screamed lustily at the male models who sashayed down the dance floor bare chested in Salman Khan Ishtyle. It was hot... hot... hot as models walked down the discotheque in Levis jeans, which are to be worn below the navel. Doesn't matter if the button is undone to give just the right glimpse. Make sure the zip is locked.

To be honest, the show put up by wonder boy from Bangalore Prasad Bidappa was terrific. Mark Robinson gave the final touch to the show as Rohit Bal, Delhi's designer guru looked on with interest. "In case you are interested," says Bidappa, "the Levis goes very well with your personality attributes, whether it is like the rugged animal of the jungle or even the black sheep, it surely is going to fit to perfection." Levis is available in which are to be worn special sizes and colour for the Indian ladies, including one that is designed to be worn with boots.

Ticklish Issues and an Ambassador-at-large

There is a subtle diplomacy being practised by the honorary councils of various countries in India who happen to be successful businessmen. Like in the ease of Vivek Burman, who represents Nicaragua in this category of envoys and is also the managing director of Dabur group of companies. Nicaragua is one of the largest states of central America and very sparsely populated.

Burman is as popular in the diplomatic circle as perhaps his products are in the country. He hosted the last monthly lunch for the deputy heads of mission and minister counsellors recently. Usually there is always somebody from the South Block who attends these meetings. It was the Director, Passports and Visas, Ms Saha this time.

Unlike the usual get together at cocktails and national day parties where the crowd is so large that you can just manage only a nod even to the most familiar ones, there is direct interaction among the diplomats -

both Indian and foreign leading to useful exchange of information in such meetings.

In this case a question-answer session at the end of the lunch dealt with visas for dependents, foreign prisoners in different prisons across the country wanting to change or waiting deportation etc. formed the most interesting part of the informal lunch. All the questions were answered patiently by the Director, Passport and Visa who many-a-times had to remind the diplomats that India is a very big country and has its own regulations. Especially in the case of foreign criminals which involves the police as well.

On many occasions recognising the nationality of the criminal itself was a huge problems. What do you do if you are just sent an audio cassette of the criminal from some part of the country requesting you to identify the nationality of the person? Well, here's a real diplomatic problem!

While many diplomats posted here write about their stint in India without of course failing to mention, about the popular Pushkar mela in Rajasthan cit is a must in almost every diplomat's itinery), there is one ambassador who has churned out a book on his country.

Somalian ambassador Mohammed Osman Omar's second book on the ethnic war raging in Somalia tilled *Somalia: A Nation driven to Despair* is a personal account of records and events that has taken place in his country. At time he reflects sadly on these events and at times angrily. His first book *The Road to Zero, Somalia's Self Destruction* was a reasonable success, most of which was written when the civil war was on in Somalia. He writes easily with a lucid flow. His book is a painstaking account of the western forces who are trying to impose their own model of democracy on his ethnically strife torn country. With virtually no government in his country, Mohammed is an ambassador-at-large trying to keep the moral of his fellow countrymen high, not only in India but in all parts of the world. He is one of the most active ambassador in New Delhi dividing his time between lawn tennis, seminars and cocktails despite being a teetotaler.

Ambassador Mohammed is a man of many talents, writing being just one of them. Though, when and how he gets the time to write despite his busy schedule is a mystery. And then again he could a teach a thing or two to budding chefs, his pastas and lasagnas he makes the flat noodles himself are mouthwatering and his pizzas are out of this world.

I still remember when I couldn't make it to his house one particular evening he had sent me the delicious pizza all packed and full of cheese. When I met him next he was showing me the bottled lime and chilly pickles stacked neatly in his kitchen shelf. "They are for some my lady ambassador friends," he said. Somalia is not an exception when it comes to countries with disputed status back home. Sahrawi Republic is another example of a embassy without a formal ambassador and a government. Despite rooftop sympathetic proclamations by successive governments.

New Delhi is yet to send the agreement for the acceptance of a ambassador of Sahrawi. Surprisingly enough leaders like Gujral Indrajit Gupta and Surjeet were in the vanguard of Indian support to Sahrawi's request for a full fledged ambassador when they were in opposition. It is obvious that the South Block mandarins call the shots when it comes to ticklish diplomatic issue. Here the deterrent factor being the Moroccan opposition in particular and the division of OIC members in general over the status of Sahrawi.

Another example is Taiwan which has been allowed to open trade mission in Vasant Vihar despite no formal diplomatic relation between the two countries. Gone are the days when India was in dilemma over Chinese

Achilles heels like Taiwan and Tibet. Today India is maintaining a respectable distance and a formidable posture with all parties concerned.

It's time to Befriend Again

Gujral dispatched his trusted nephew Ajay Singh (remember journalist-turned politician who was deputy railways minister in VP Singh government and who has Fijian connections both from his late father and former Indian high commissioner Bhagwan Singh and wife's side) on a secret mission to the South Pacific island of Fiji, he was prompted to do so because of the sudden developments in the 800-strong Melensian archipelage almost half of whose one million population is of Indian origin.

Hutchinson encyclopaedia tells me that only a decade ago it was 54 per cent but after the two successive coups in 1987 (one unsuccessful in April but second time successful in September), led by then colonel and now general Sitiveni Rabuka (trained in India) forced all those Indians who had a flicker of hope for greener pastures to flee. Today the figure stands at unconfirmed 46 per cent. But this innocuous arithmetical figure doesn't tell the whole story.

Measuring 18,337 square kilometres, Fiji consisted of short but stoutly built Micronesian, Polynesian and Melanesian tribals who until the ship 'Ganges' carrying indentured Indians sailed into Suva on the main island Vitilevu on June 27, 1885. The land belonged to the indigenous but was leased out to Indians on long-term basis after their indenture contract was over. Everything was hunky dory till politics arrived on the scene. The outnumbered aboriginals were led to believe that if some fire-fighting was not done, Fiji would become a mini India in the Pacific. By that time, fishermen in troubled waters such as Malaysia had arrived on the scene who not only invested heavily but also propounded the theory of the son of soil.

However, Indians are largely to be blamed for this situation. Because even after a century of stay, they couldn't mix with the local people and maintained their own cultural identity. At this point, a mention of the role played by our successive; high commissioners such as Sonu Kocher and TP Sreenivasan must be made who added fuel to the fire by siding with the debatable causes of Indians rather than the genuine concerns of the Fijians as a whole.

Rabuka's military coup snatched the majority status of Indians, reducing them to 27 seats in a representative lower house of 70. A furious India prevailed upon Britain and other Commonwealth members to exclude Fiji from the club. This situation lasted for about a decade. In this period many things happened.

The predominant tribal chiefs started missing the halo of the British crown which was a source of reflected glory for them. With Indian exodus and growing indifference in their economy especially in the sugar sector, Rabuka has realised that there is no choice but to bring them back in the political mainstream. Hence he has introduced sweeping constitutional amendments which will restore electoral rights to Indians to contest for the highest offices in the land. Political leaders such as Jairam Reddy have played a significant role in changing the scenario for the benefit of Indians. The upper house senate dominated by tribal chiefs has relented in the hope that Indian would not lift diplomatic pressure against Fiji and let it return to commonwealth. For last 10 years, there has been no diplomatic relations between the two countries, though Indians arriving on Klandy airport have been granted transit and tourist visas.

Various Hindu outfits have been visiting Fiji to espouse the cause of their brethren who had left the motherland 100 years ago. There overtures should be discouraged. Such fissiparous tendencies have created problems for people of Indian origin from Mauritius to the Caribbean. One such self-styled Hindu protagonist was refused audience by Rabuka when he heard about his Vivekananda-style clarion call for rise, awake and be enlightened against the demons (local tribals).

My dear friend Ajay Singh had been sent into this background to assess and report the ground situation. He is a very enlightened and sharp mediator who should be able to handle the delicate task. There were still two years to go for Rabuka's amended constitution to come in operation then India should not wait to reciprocate the gesture and use all diplomatic skills to win back a lost friend in the larger interest of half-a-million people who were Indians a couple of generation ago.

While on the subject, a reference to the neighbouring South Pacific islands including Nauru, Kiribati, Tavalu, Western Samoa, Cook and Tonga, Neu as well as Solomon and Vanuatu will not be out of place. Most of them are either members of commonwealth, the UN or its front organisations. Islands such as Tonga have a lot of goodwill for India. They still remember Mrs. Gandhi's visit. Nehru even has a honorary consulate general KS Bhatia in New Delhi. According to Japanese experts, by 2020 they will be the centre of global attention because of their rich marine, minerals and aromatic and herbal value based products. Not only Australia and New Zealand, but even Malaysia, Indonesia, China and even the US have arrived with their shipping and mining company to exploit the vast treasures hidden under the sea. India, through technical cooperation programme, can easily befriend them as a part of its 'look east' policy. Now when it has been made a member of ASEAN regional forum and a dialogue partner of ASEAN, its time we look towards Fiji and the adjoining island nations.

On Firm Economic Footing

The Sultan of Oman is coming to India at a very opportune time next week. The visit close on the heels of the recent launching of the Indian Ocean Rim Association for Regional Cooperation (IOR-ARC) at Port Louis in Mauritius earlier this month marks a new era in Indo-Omani relations opening new avenues in shipping linkages and port facilities.

The visit of Sultan Qaboos Bin Said Al Said to India has many firsts. We are told it is his first not only to India but to any other Asian or non-Muslim country towards the east of Oman. It is his reciprocal gesture of India and its President Shankar Dayal Sharma whose state visit last year was overwhelming on more accounts than one. However, India is not unfamiliar either to the Sultan of Oman. His grandfather lay buried in a private royal cemetery in Bombay where he breathed his last during the British raj when Oman was ruled by the British regent of Bombay. Sultan's family has deep-rooted linkages with India. Many members of his cabinet have roots in other cities including Hyderabad. The royal family apart, Oman is bound with India through history spanning over 3,000 years. It is replete with the aroma of sandalwood, shine of precious stones and the tenacity of copper. There are reasons to believe that Vasco de Gama would not have reached India but for Omani navigator Ahmed bin Majid. The story of Tipu Sultan would have been less colourful if he did not have close relations with Oman. No wonder the largest expatriate community in Oman is formed by Indians. Mumbai and Muscat were connected by sea and air during the British times. This continued even after India got Independence. One of the first visitors to the first Indian governor general C Rajgopalachari was the representative the then Sultan of Oman.

The relationship between India and Oman was manifest in factors including the Indian rupee being the legal tender in the country till 1960s, treaty of friendship signed in 1953 and cooperation in oil and hydrocarbon sectors. Oman and India have actively cooperated in fora such as the NAM. There is not a single factor on either side which could impede the growth of a sustained and harmonious relationship. There have been series of high level bilateral visits starting from Indian Foreign minister Swaran Singh's journey in 1974, India and Japan are connected by air with a sizable traffic on both sides.

Federation of Indian Chamber of Commerce and Industry (FICCI) has been interacting with Oman for last two decades in capital goods as well as durables and non-durables. An company designed and developed the township of Sohar and its port facilities. Today, a very large number of construction, consultancy and trading companies are engaged in the export of electronics, trucks and buses. But much more can be done.

India and Oman were ready to sign three important agreements during Sultan's visit. They include avoidance of double taxation, protection of trade and investment as well as an extradition treaty. India could also discuss the areas of mutual cooperation under the umbrella of recently launched multi-lateral forum IORARC which is being touted as a landmark in 35 odd littoral states washed by the blue waters of Indian ocean. Incidentally, India and Oman happen to be the founder members of this regional grouping which binds Asia and Africa with Oceania.

Gulf region has always been an important factor in India's foreign policy initiatives, both on account of oil and Muslim response to our domestic developments pertaining our large minority community. Thankfully, Oman has always been appreciative of issues including Kashmir and Babri Masjid. Despite Pakistan's manipulations of Organisation Islamic Countries (OIC), we continue to bank upon the support of friends such as Oman.

It is purely coincidental that the Sultan's visit was followed by the OIC foreign ministers' conference in Islamabad next week where the host might be tempted again to queer the pitch for the long awaited meeting between the foreign secretaries of Pakistan and India in the last week of March. Needless to say, the bilateral talks between India and Oman will provide an golden opportunity to brief and influential member of OIC on India's desire and efforts to normalise relations with our neighbour. India and Oman's mutual trust is conspicuous in the shared, regional security concerns and the consequent reassuring efforts through joint naval exercises, hydrographic surveys and training of Omani coast guards.

This trust extends in other realms of culture and education through bilateral agreements but the cornerstone remains the economic agenda which includes joint economic commission, joint business council, Most Favoured Nation (MFN) treatment, petroleum, and fertiliser joint projects. Sultan's present visit will also augment the air linkages through more flights and destinations.

But the most pressing need is to correct the imbalance in the bilateral trade (140,27,27.09 US $ million) which is heavily in favour of India. If this visit could till the balance in favour of Oman, a long standing irritant could be removed. Though Oman's imports from India stood at Rs 36,347.89 lakh last financial year, still it is only 3.3 per cent of its total import.

That is a different matter that despile this, India is the fifth largest exporter to Oman after the US, Japan, Germany, UK and Saudi Arabia. Indian exports include textiles, meat, electric and electronic appliances, rice, manufactured goods, machinery and transport equipment, tea, coffees and rubber. Oman has so us a long list of goods which could be imported among other things. The ammonia urea fertiliser project with a production capacity of 1.45 million tonnes of urea and 300,000 tonnes of ammonia set up in Sur will offset the imbalance to a large extent.

The bilateral trade can grow to mutual advantage if there is a better and bigger participation in trade fairs, standardisation of testing of export items like pesticides and drugs, bartering of oil with traditional items like tea, rice and meat, lifting of ban on Indian livestock, legalisation and authetication of export documents at places other than Delhi-Mumbai and facilitating business visas could help a lot.

Oman has already taken an initiative in frequent ship-line. If India could reciprocate it by reducing its average tariff of 27 per cent as against 5 per cent of Oman to bring it to more rational international level, the tone and texture of bilateral relations could be put on a firm economic looting.

Prodigal Visits Fatherland

Trinidad and Tobago Prime Minister Basdeo Panday was the guest of honour at the Republic Day celebrations on 50th year of Indian Independence. Panday's presence on the Republic Day in the 50th year of Indian Independence was significant because he was the first Prime Minister of Indian origin the English-speaking South American country which has 41 per cent population whose forefathers had migrated from eastern Uttar Pradesh and western Bihar 150 years ago as indentured labour to work in the British owned sugarcane fields.

Trinidad and Tobago has a population of 12 lakhs in which the majority 59 per cent is of African descent who had originally come as slaves at different points of history. Thus this two-island nation on the north-west tip of South America, popularly known as Latin America, represents a unique multi-ethnic and multi-cultural secular society. Prime Minister Panday shared his experiences with his Indian audience at India International Centre on January 25 as how did they achieve this distinction. Panday will be the second successive executive head of state from that region to be our guest on January 26. Last year, it was Brazilian President Fernando Henriquez Cardoso. It speaks volumes about the efforts India is making to reach out to the region. Panday hails from the Lakshmanpur village of Azamgarh district in Uttar Pradesh where the nephew of his grandfather still lives with his family. He visited them on January 27 after participating in the R-Day festivities. He was in India visiting many cities including Agra, Varanasi (where he will be conferred) upon a honorary doctorate by Banaras Hindu University.

Incidentally, he graduated in law from Lincoln's Inn and has a diploma in drama from London School of Dramatic Art after starting his professional life as cane weigher and then as a primary school teacher.

His presence in India on our R-Day should be seen as a visit of prodigal to his fatherland, a phenomenon which has been a thorny issue in Indian foreign policy pursuits. There are at least four countries viz. Surinam, Guyana on the Atlantic coast, apart from Trinidad and Tobago along with Mauritius in Indian Ocean and Fiji in the Pacific, which have decisive presence of the people of Indian origin.

How should India deal with this populace which is culturally and religiously attached to the umbilical cord but for all practical purposes are foreign nationals has always been a ticklish issue for South Block. Any overzealous overture is found to be misunderstood by other ethnic communities as has happened in Fiji, Mauritius, Guyana and even Surinam at different points of their political histories. Thankfully, it has not happened in case of Trinidad and Tobago.

It was always a debating point in that country what will happen when and if a prime minister of Indian origin takes over. Recently, after one year of his prime ministership, Panday told a select audience of prospective investors in New York that whenever he made a bid for power, he was told that the time had not come for with an experiment because the country was not ready to accept such a leader. It was apprehended that he would not be fair and impartial with other communities.

He dared his detractors to give one example of racial discrimination. Though as a leader of opposition, he was considered to be a rabid pro-India and Indian, causing some discomfort to New Delhi, but it has been proved beyond doubt that that was just a political rhetoric expected of an aspirant for the top job in any country. However, after taking over in November 1995, he was a changed man displaying all the finer qualities of a statesman.

Surprisingly, such an issue doesn't bother any other country in the world. It is not that large masses of humanity have not crossed oceans in search of livelihood or by force of history.

The best example is of Africans from the eastern coast like Sierra Leone but they don't crave for their roots like Indians do. I am not talking about those Indians who left on their own in this century from Gujarat and Sindh, which is now in Pakisthan, for cast African nations such as Uganda, Kenya and Tanzania after their predecessor's had shown them the way to El Dorado, but those who were drafted as indentured labour and put in a ship for an unknown destination, started from scratch and are playing a meaningful role in the polity and economy of that country.

The former category is always on the verge of being asked to leave, as has been in case in Uganda and

Tanzania, while the latter is an integral part of the present political and economic dispensation.

Today, it is the considered opinion of all and sundry engaged in the art of diplomacy that gone are the days when we continue to harp on age old cultural and religious linkages.

During my four-day stay in that country as a part of the President Shankar Dayal Sharma's encourage in June1995, when he was invited to the commemoration of the 150th anniversary of Indian arrival in that country, I interacted with a lot of college students of Indian origin.

None of them had visited India but only heard stories from their parents and grandparents. I didn't find any great love lost for India or Indians except a nodding acquaintance at the mention of this country. They won't mind in coming to India, but only as tourists. This mindset is quite different from that of some of us here, who keep on playing the tune of our long lost brethren who must be restored to their roots.

Today, we have to speak in the language of business. While doing that, our historical relations could be a point of reference but nothing more than that. That is why we have no problem in dealing with the present day non-resident Indians whom we keep on inviting to come and invest here.

It is the other way round in the countries where there is a large population of Indian origin. Prime Minister Basdeo Panday is bringing a large business delegation with him and he will be addressing a lunch-on meeting organised by CII in Delhi and similar meetings elsewhere in the country during his 12-days sojourn in India.

There is a great scope for Indian investors in the manufacturing sector in the field of Pharmaceuticals, computer software, textiles, energy, agro-based products and food processing. The Mittal Group of Calcutta known for their Ispat (steel) collaborations in far flung areas from

Mexico to Kazakhstan have shown the way by their management of the Ispat, Caribbean plant in the capital city of Port of Spain.

Like in the case of almost every Latin American country, the US is major trading partner of Trinidad and Tobago, but the latter has a special arrangement with neighbouring Venezuela and Columbia. It is a member of CARICOM (Caribbean Community of English speaking around the Caribbean sea) which has linkages with the Latin American grouping of MERCOSUR countries (Brazil, Argentina, Uruguay and Paraguay), CARICOM has a combined market of five million people. It is also the founder member of the newly formed ACS (Association of Caribbean States), with its headquarters in Port of Spain. ACS has a combined GDP of 500 million US $ and population of 200 million. It is also trying to be a member of NAFTA (North American Free Trade Association). Though it is a young nation having attained independence in 1962 only and small too with a population of 12 lakhs, but has a high literacy rate of 90 per cent, impeccable record of human rights and no holds barred economy for foreign investors provides an excellent gateway to Indian entrepreneur for western hemisphere.

We have had many guests of honour in past too and also Latin American but Basdeo Panday is a very special person for India for the above-mentioned reasons. We should not fritter away this opportunity for fostering and consolidating our traditional ties through the modern lingua franca of trade and commerce ties.

When a Prime Minister Travelled into History

The life of a tiny village Lakhmanpur Patti Badalrai in Azamgarh is not same since when a native returned to the land of his forefathers who had left if exactly 90 years ago in a ship called Fatai Razzak from the Kolkata port to a future which they hoped - would definitely better their existing lot which was next to nothing. They were not very wrong. It is a different mailer that at least two generations had to go through slavery, drudgery and discrimination. But a century later, one of them is the prime minister of Trinidad and Tobago, Basdeo Panday.

Only time will tell whether it was a judicious decision on the part of prime minister Panday to send the researcher Shamsuddeen as an advance party to locate his lost village and roots in Azamgarh district. This search reminded me of a story I had read a couple of years ago about an Indian indentured labourer who left newly-wedded wife in "ghunghat" and the name Trinidad as his forwarding address. A couple of years later he met a woman with a child working with him side by side in a sugar plantation in Port of Spain who had come to Trinidad looking for his husband. Like that woman, Panday also succeeded in locating his cousins and nephews and gave them a crore of rupees, courtesy Trinidad businessmen who had accompanied him to India. Before Panday's arrival, Lakhmanpur was a sleepy village where Yadavs and bhoomihars lived amidst hostility. The latter had snatched the land and the homes including the ones which were supposed to be the ancestral abode of the prime minister's family. The moment the news of the newly found relationship with a prime minister became public, the Yadavs hoped that the visiting dignitary would be able to get them back their land and homes. But that was not to be. The reunion after 90 years was an emotional one, with tears flowing from both the sides. When the prime minister composed himself, he realised the Pandora's box he had opened. He gave enough, promised more and left. Perhaps never to return.

The prime minister would go back to his adopted country in the Caribbean and occasionally relate his journey to his fatherland, but the poor country cousins would not be same for the rest of their lives. The prime minister proudly announced that the Indian immigrants had left their castes behind in India. That explains how he became a high caste Panday from a Yadav, but he can't change the caste of his newly-found cousins who are destined to live as Yadavs for all times to come in the menacing company of bhoomihars.

It will always be debated in India and Trinidad what purpose was served by this laborious exercise undertaken by a foreign prime minister who happens to be of India descent. He might have fulfilled a personal desire. But it has raised questions about the ideal relationship people of Indian origin should have with their fatherland. Frankly speaking, there is no love lost between the present generation of the people of Indian origin and India. This is true not only about Trinidad, but also about Fiji, Mauritius, Guyana, Surinam and Jamaica. In fact, the Indian connection of this significant population in these countries has proved to be disadvantageous because the equally strong African-origin population sans any traceable roots have always doubled their integrity and Indian intention. Even Panday had to wait for three decades for becoming the first prime minister of his country with Indian roots.

Indians had taken an excessively large cultural and religious baggage with them a century and a half ago when they were drafted as indentured labour. This has not allowed them to grow harmoniously with the rest of the people in the new country. This situation is quite different from Africans in these countries and even Europeans anywhere in the world. The best example is the United States which consists of none else but immigrants from all parts of the world. It is a common knowledge that only Indians and Pakistanis retain their cultural and religious identity causing incidents like dot busting in the US and the Paki bashing in the UK.

The late prime minister of Mauritius Sir Shewsagar Ramgoolam also came to Azamgarh looking for his native village two decades ago and the life for people of Indian origin in his country became difficult. That is why Indian government has maintained a respectable distance from the politicians of Indian origin in the Caribbean and elsewhere. But Panday has stirred a hornet's nest by his pilgrimage. Incidentally, a colourful and beautiful carnival, conceived and presented by Anita Chandradutt Singh, wife of the chief of protocol of Trinidad at Darbar Hall of hotel Taj Palace last week, was the true picture of Trinidad. We hope and pray that the emotional outburst of the prime minister doesn't disturb the rainbow colours when he returns home after a week.

3
Bilateral Taste of Pudding

Dalai Birthday to be a Private Affair

Government of India decided to look the other way when Dalai Lama celerates his 60th birthday at Ashoka Hotel here from July 4 to 6.

South Block is aware of the fact that as relations between New Delhi and Beijing are smoothening it will be diplomatically unwise to give these celebrations any kind of official patronage.

The celebrations included four symposia non-political themes like "Non-violence, compassion and visions for the 21st century", "Time and Transcendence," Inner and Outer Disciplines" and "Divergence and Convergence of Sciences and Spirituality". But there seems to be a subtle move to involve people like former President R. Venkataraman, former Congress President S. Nijalingappa, Sundar Lal Bahuguna, Raja Ramanna and Jayant Vishnu Narlikar.

Incidentally, the reception committee was headed by National Human Rights Commission chairman Justice Raghunath Mishra who refused to be drawn in any controversy whether his present dispensation has any thing to do with human rights abuse in Dalai Lama's land Tibet.

Neither the Government of India nor the Dalai Lama's Government-in-exile based at Dharamsala in Himachal Pradesh has been formally invited to the celebrations but anyone in his personal capacity is welcome, said Justice Mishra last evening at a Press conference in Ashoka Hotel.

According to another reception committee member and a former secretary in the Ministry of External Affairs, Lakhan Mahrotra, this was the first time when Dalai Lama's birthday is being celebrated at such a level where participants from Germany, Russia and other CIS countries, England, Poland, Japan, USA, Canada, Australia, Switzerland, Malaysia, South Korea, Abu Dhabi, Nepal, Kenya, Sri Lanka and France. One explanation is that 60th birthday is the beginning of third phase in Indian interpretation of life cycle.

Gaping Holes

The backyard of Myanmar's embassy in India ironically represents the present state of its bilateral relations with India. The uneven and uncut wild grass separating the chaneery and the residential block is reminiscent of the fungus which has engulfed our mutual perception ignoring the age old historical link between the two neighbours.

Though Indian Airlines has started bi-weekly flights between Calcutta and Rangoon and there is a perceptible interest among Indian traders for exploring business possibilities, but there are gaping holes in India's policy towards Myanmar, still known as Burma in Indian common parlance. Though India continues to be the popular divine destination for salvation seeking Burmese Buddhist pilgrims who account for the entire tourist traffic on board Indian Airlines, but there is no reciprocity on the part of Indian tourists, religious or otherwise. And there seems to be no effort on the part of Indian Airlines to popularise this route either through Buddhist circuit or among lakhs of Indians who have made Myanmar their home for good.

Myanmar is interwoven with Indian history through the last Moghul emperor Bahadur Shah Zafar who lies buried there, albeit not so peacefully if you go by the reports filed by Indian journalists who were on board the inaugural flight to Rangoon from Calcutta. But then, that seems to be the order of the day reflecting our indifference towards the history of subcontinent as similar is the fate of the mausoleum of the legendary queen of Awadh (present day Lucknow) Begum Hazrat Mahal in Kathmandu, Nepal and the grave of the founder of Mughal empire in India Babar in Kabul Afghanistan. However, that is another story.

Coming back to Indian attitudinal neglect of Myanmar and the overzealous support to the so-called democracy movement in that country seems to be governed by the western yardstick measuring human rights and freedom movements. With due respect to the nobel peace laureate Aung Suu Kyi, who was hardly 16 months old in her domestic politics when she was decorated with this highly controversial and politicised award, we seem to have ignored the basic five tenets of peaceful co-existence called Panchsheel, governing bilateral relations between any two sovereign nations.

What is happening in Myanmar is their internal matter. They know best about the form of government suitable to their local conditions which is highly infested with insurgency and underground movements like India. Myanmar has over 130 communities vying for their due or undue slice in the national cake. Myanmar is sandwiched between two geographically and militarily large nations, namely India and China, both of which are haven for their dissidents. It has a ripple effect on our north-east and the corresponding counterpart of China. No wonder Nehru and Indira Gandhi maintained more than cordial relations with the regime of general Ne Win despite his uniformed dispensation.

But one doesn't know at which point of history, the Indian perception about Myanmar got westernised and we started distancing ourselves from the friendly rulers of Myanmar. We even allowed our sensitive establishments like the news division of All India Radio to be the nucleus of anti-Myanmar activities. Incidentally, the daughter of a former prime minister and later a secretary general of the UN, UN heads the Burmese news section, thereby giving more than necessary coverage to the dissident activities both in India and Myanmar. We have already burnt our fingers in case of Tibetan refugees which has proved detrimental to Sino-India relations and now when even Dalai Lama has realised that Tibetan freedom is an Utopia and we don't know-how to contain his lakhs of followers who have developed deeprooted economic interests in India. Today, Dalai wants to shift his base to some western capital but his kinsmen don't want to leave India.

Though the situation is not that grave in case of Burmese dissidents whose number has not touched four figures but their continuous inflow through the porous Indo-Burma border could turn into a serious situation. These dissidents manage to get an easy passage into India and then they fan out in different parts of the country trying to raise the flag of revolt as and when the situation demands. There are many NGOs (Non-governmental organisations) funded by international agencies who generously finance these activities in case of Afghanistan, Iran, Palestine, Sudan and Bangladesh. And look where we have reached. We don't have best of relations with any of these countries. The recent voting pattern in the election to the non-permanent seat for security council and our humiliating defeat has proved beyond doubt that our foreign policy is not governed by national interest. Gone are the days of non-aligned and the natural Indian leadership. Today, we have to build each bilateral relationship on individual merit. And Myanmar could be a good beginning. Otherwise, any number of Indian Airlines flights would prove to be flights.

East-west Divide in South Block

The Ministry of External Affairs (MEA) is always ill-at-ease because of its next door neighbours—the omnipotent Prime Minister's Office (PMO) on its east and the ever-proliferating Defence on its west. Literally and figuratively, the MHA is sandwiched between the two. Even if it desires, it can't wish away the former. It has however managed to slight the latter at every given opportunity. In fact when it wanted to punish one of its most intelligent officers for calling a spade a spade, it shifted him to defence thinking they were dumping him, but he has bounced, back with flying colours.

The subject of this week's column, Lt Gen Satish Nambiar and though him the United Nations Peace Keeping Force (UNPKF) is yet another example of how the MHA chooses (ignore) the lessons drawn by one of India's biggest diplomatic initiatives undertaken in the world's highest forum by putting the lives of thousands of our officers and men at risk.

A highly decorated and experienced general, Nambiar has the unique honour of having served as the first force commander and head of mission, of the United Nations forces in Bosnia (former Yugoslavia). After exactly one year, he preferred to call it a day rather than be virtually demoted to number two position in the same force which he had commanded with rare distinction under the most difficult conditions. Then he headed the prestigious United Service Institution of India as its director and has been invited to speak at home and abroad on his Bosnia assignment except by the MEA which either doesn't bother about the plight of the co-founder Non-

Aligned Movement (NAM) any longer or is complacent with its know all attitude. In fact that has been the fate of all such initiatives taken by experts other than Indian Foreign Service (IFS) personnel. Only the other clay, the India International Centre invited the former Water Resources Secretary to speak on his experiences in Yemen. The former foreign secretary Salman Haider had requested him to got to the Gulf nation and study the fast developing water crisis there and perhaps suggest a management strategy before the small Gulf nation runs out of water. I could see the horror writ large on the face of the guest speaker when he realised that he would be speaking to five people in total. And none of them belonged to MHA or the Yemen embassy who were his sponsors and hosts respectively. Anyhow coming back to my subject, the sum total of our Bosnian odyssey was that everything is not right with the UNPKF. More often than not no preparations are made before deciding to send multinational forces into troubled waters. No study is made about, the ground realities which, many a times change with lightning speed as it happened in the case of Bosnia. Then there are perception and communication gaps between the UN headquarters and the mission on how to conduct operations at the trouble spot. There is also the obvious western bias against the east which results in change of command and staff. There is no time frame to complete the assignment. There are varying views on the sovereignty of the State or States concerned, which in turn leads many times to knee-jerk reactions.

But that doesn't mean in the fast changing global scenario UNPKF doesn't have the potential to play a major constructive role. And India will continue to play an important role as it has done in Cyprus, Gaza, Somalia, Haiti, Angola, Congo, Lebanon, West Iran, Yemen, Kuwait, Rwanda, Iran-Iraq, and Kampuchea. Thousands of Indian men and hundreds of our officers have participated and many have laid down their lives for the cause of world peace.

But a debate is on at various levels now on whether India's position and clout in the world body is in justified proportion to our consistent contribution, which has incidentally been universally accepted and making a serious bid for a permanent Security Council seat in the restructured UNO, should we not ask for our rightful position in decision-making and implementation.

If the US can ask for deducting its shared cost of the peace-keeping operations from its voluntary contribution which it makes to meet its political and strategic designs, so can we.

Finally, the Indian establishment should seriously consider General Nambiar's suggestion of asking the UN to set up a training centre for UN peace-keeping forces in India so that its operations could be streamlined and not ad hoc as they are at the moment.

Pakistan Scores Yet Another Diplomatic First

Pakistan has gone through to one of the most turbulent polls in its chequered history dominated by military dispensations and ethnic violence. Still it has shown the courage of inviting 400-odd international election observers including a dozen from India. The latter has never agreed to such requests cither from the developed West nor from the developing East, not to mention the inimical neighbourhood. There was no compulsion for Islamabad to accede to the suggestion made by the Colombo-based international institute ethnic studies devoted to SAARC countries in particular and the rest in general. But the president Leghari and the caretaker Prime Minister Khalid of Pakistan felt the pressing need to show the world that a decisive section of Pakistani polity and intelligentsia is still interested in proving the point that Islamic nation is genuinely democratic.

These elections not only sealed the fake of the Bhutto legacy in Pakistan but will also settle the choice for governance. Pakistani army, which has been restive in its barracks seeing the shoddy games the country's civilian leaders are playing with each other and the country, may not wait for too long if the democracy fails this time.

That is why when the institute asked Islamabad if it could organise 10 impartial apolitical poll observers each from SAARC countries to observe the electoral process and report to the world about its fairness and authenticity, Pakistan readily agreed.

The institute was established by a local Sri Lankan MP and now run by bis enthusiastic son Jeewan which has done remarkable job in analysing and offering solutions to the knotty ethnic problems like Hindu-Muslim, Sia-Sunni, Simhala-Tamil, Bhutanese-Nepalese, Chakmas, Bangladeshis refugees et al. The former foreign secretary of India Muchkund Duney who has also been chosen to comprise the Indian team told this columnist that it was very brave on the part of the present regime across the border to accept Indian participation in this international exercise aimed at promoting democratic processes the world over.

Why did he not impress upon his next door neighbour PMO in South Block for such observers. Dubey replied with a vague smile.

Obviously India didn't feel the need for international observers to ensure that elections here were free and fair especially when the big brother Seshan was watching. But Seshan was an individual and the electoral process is an institution and India should have at least agreed in case of Punjab now five years ago when the state went to the polls after a decade of Pakistan sponsored low-cost war against India through militant insurgency. All the charges that elections in Punjab were a managed affair would have fallen flat much before the next year's which witnessed the return of peace despile the low turn-out at the hustings.

Similarly, the recently held election in Kashmir was yet another opportunity to invite international observers including Red Cross that at least we were sincere in attempting a popularly elected government in the militancy-infested Valley. But India has never agreed to expose the internal situation in Punjab or Kashmir to the international public opinion under the pretext of such observers are prejudiced to begin with.

This approach has given credence to lie fact that we have something to hide in our governance of these states. On just score, Pakistan has more to sweep under its carpel by inviting Indian and other observers.

It has scored yet another diplomatic victory over India. This columnist Jeil the same when he was allowed to visit the Pakistan occupied Kashmir in the heydays of the training camps in 1990. Not that all Kashmiri separatists spoke in favour of merging with Pakistan after she 'Azadi.'

Lessons from Argentina Nuclear policy

India is under great pressure from the US to sign a Comprehensive Test Ban Treaty (CTBT). This pressure has heightened after the President Clinton's visit. Since then American officials, and diplomats do not forget to impress upon India on this core at all fora they speak from.

Americans generally give the example of Argentina and Brazil who signed the treaty of Talatelolco to establish the world first nuclear weapon free zone and system of international control of national nuclear facilities through a permanent supervisory organ.

The American argument is that if Argentina and Brazil could enter into such a arrangement why can't India and Pakistan follow this example.

This Brazilian Left Won't go Right

Left of the centre political leaders in Latin America have been seen crossing over to the right when confronted with the ground economic realities. Delhi hasted the vice president of the Brazilian senate Ademir Andrade who stopped over in the Capital en route Beijing at the invitation of the Chinese communist party. Here also he made it a point to call on the Indian communist leaders of various hues and shades.

To begin with this is an interesting development that a Latin American political leader is visiting Asian capitals presumably to strengthen the leftist network. Otherwise Latinos have never minced words in publicly stating their preference for Taiwan over China.

But more fascinating was listening to him after a reception in the Vintage Mandarin restaurant of Janpath Hotel where he claimed that the real left was round the corner to capture power in Brazil.

Before reporting senator Andrade in greater details, allow me to be a bit nostalgic about the Mandarin.

One doesn't know-how much more time the Vajpayee government would give to Indian public sector hotels before the auction hammer is struck in the disinvestments market. Thus it was a Jadeja for old timers like me and the host Daulat Singhji P Jadeja of Indian Society for Latin America (ISLA) who appeared to be nostalgic about the place.

Jadeja's ISLA is credited for introducing Latin America to Indian parliamentarians in particular and the rest of the people in general. According to its secretary, Prof Abdul Nafey, ISLA is running 28 and is known for hosting the Latin American dignitaries whenever they pass by Delhi, besides organising seminars, publishing books and creating a political constituency for Indo-Latin American relations.

Coming back to the guest of the afternoon, the veteran senator belonging to Brazilian Socialist party felt that India could give a lesson or two to Brazil in agricultural production where the land reforms are yet to begin. According to him, there are individual in his country who are holding 60 million hectares of land. But despite such a big landmass, Brazil's food production was only one thirds of India's.

He was wary of the debt burden in his country and he blamed the privatisation for this.

Hope Indian champions of disinvestment are listening. He also expressed his concern at the mass exodus of the rural people to cities in Brazil.

Fourty years ago, 70 per cent Brazilians lived in the countryside. Today this ratio is only 20 per cent. The senator was surprised that despite such a vast river water resource, India was not self-sufficient in the energy sector. He offered help in this area. He advised Indians to harness the river water rather than take turns in polluting and worshipping it. He was candid to let the nuclear energy wait and hydro-electricity takeover. He said there was no need to waste fuel to produce energy.

He was conscious of the subsidy debate going on in this country. Citing the adverse impact of subsidy-cut on small and marginal farmers, he said it was suicidal and these issues should be debated before its implementation.

India has High Stakes in Hong Kong Integration

The return of Hong Kong to the mainland China on July 1, 1997 brought sweet and sour memories of Goa's coming back to Indian fold a quarter of century ago. India had to wage a minor military operation to liberate Goa from Portuguese domination. Instead China carried out a relentless diplomatic struggle for 15 years before getting back Hong Kong after a century and half of British rule. This is quite beautifully exhibited through telling photographs at the Lalit Kala gallery in Rabindra Bhawan complex at Mandi House till April 22. Unlike Portugal which left only cultural relics through beautiful churches and regal architecture in Goa, the Britons took full advantage of the oceanic placement of Hong Kong. Portuguese didn't contribute much to the economy of Goa but Hong Kong is an enviable source of international trade which was the main bone of contention between China and England.

Today, when some European and African countries are in a process of disintegration, the news from Hong Kong should bring cheers to Asians who are trying hard for regional groupings of various hues and shades such as the SAARC, ASEAN and Indian Ocean Rim. In fact, Hong Kong's strategic position at the cross-currents of Indian and Pacific oceans augurs well for the new millennium which only two and half years away.

The manner in which Hong Kong is being integrated into Chinese scheme of things speaks volumes about the shape of the things to come. Because of its vantage geography, Hong Kong has become a nucleus of shipping and information. Though China has made large investments into Hong Kong economy and vice versa, but the latter will continue to be the symbol of the new economic order which China has understandably agreed. One only hopes that the experiment of Hong Kong integration will lead to similar replication in the case of the other two jewels of the Chinese crown called Taiwan and Macau.

China has agreed for the continuation of the pre-merger contacts and relations between Taiwan and Hong

Kong, something which it doesn't accept for herself. Needless to say, Hong Kong integration is the success of Chinese diplomacy and a mild rebuff to the western mechanisations. The success of this integration should spell new hope for similar estranged geographical entities in its neighbourhood including Papua New Guinea and the two Koreas.

The developments in Hong Kong have been received with mixed reactions in India. The Gorkha community which served the British crown with unflinching loyally for 150 years and the Indian ex-patriates is apprehensive about its future. Indians have experienced similar situations elsewhere in Africa and Asia whenever the umbilical cord with the empire got snapped. At one hand it is a case of divided loyalties and on the other short-sightedness for not being able to see the writing on the wall.

Though the cosmopolitan character of Hong Kong will have sufficient room for all kinds of enterprise to survive but the interracial relations would remain a delicate issue for some time to come.

Hong Kong is not unfamiliar commodity in the post-liberalisation of India. United Airlines has conveniently connected India with the island and she Hong Kong bank has found Indian experiment quite satisfactory. The Indian presence in Hong Kong derives a lot of back up support from their linkages here. All this needs to be strengthened. In this regard, the decision to open a consulate general in Hong Kong is a welcome diplomatic move on the part of South Block. The chamber of Commerce in India should take some bold initiatives in their presence fell to promote bilateral and multilateral trade from that part of the world.

Much hue and cry has been made about the future of democracy in Hong Kong. The last vestiges of British colonial rule in the island tried to internationalise the issue by provoking the fears of Hong Kong citizens. But did Britain allow that during its domination. China has tried to allay all kinds of tears by allowing self-determination except in case of foreign, and defence matters. Not only this, it has even receded to the capitalist system operative in Hong Kong. This is a new experiment in this part of the world and nations placed in matching predicament will watch with great interest how this succeeds.

We in India, who are feeling strains on our federal structure and are in the process of resolving Kashmir issue must learn a lesson from this experiment. All large nations have to start thinking in terms of offering greater autonomy to its constituents if they want to retain their existing boundaries. Otherwise, the fates of the then Soviet Union and Yugoslavia are not too remote. Lastly, one only wishes if the self-styled leaders of the Tibetan autonomy also take a cue from Hong Kong and join heads to end the miseries of millions of their brethren who are compelled to lead a nomadic life.

When it Comes to Sahara, Even Gujral, Surjeet, Gupta have no Say

It is shocking yet truce even the then ruling trio of home minister Inderjit Gupta, Foreign minister IK Gujral and the CPM Supremo Harkishan Singh Surjeet in 1997 could not invite the Saharan ambassador. These three had argued with the then Rao government to invite the new Saharan ambassador but South Block prevailed upon the then political leadership against this and continues to do so even now. What could be the reason?

Even after 21 years of independence proclaimed by Popular Front for the liberation of the Saguiet El Humra and Rio de Oro (Polisario), Western Sahara continues to be the last post of colonialism despite the active intervention of the international community and dozens of UN resolutions.

Surprisingly enough, since 1976, 75 countries, including India, have recognised the Saharawi republic. Still its two-third area is under the fortified possession of Morocco. About 165,000 of its people are in the refugee camps in the friendly neighbourhood of Algeria. Hundreds of them have died while fighting a guerrilla war and many more are missing. Not even a single country, including the members of the Organisation of African Unity (OAU), has accepted the so-called historical claim of Morocco over Saharawi territory. The international court of justice reaffirmed the Saharawi right of self-determination in 1975. Following two years of hectic diplomatic activity by the UN and OAU, a settlement plan was drawn to end the conflict in 1988 which called for a referendum between integration with Morocco and independence. But a stalemate continues over the voting right. Morocco wants the entire five million residents in the occupied territory to participate in the referendum while Saharawis claim that when Spain left, the population of their country was only 64,000. Thereby meaning that the additional people are those Moroccans who have been forcibly settled to tilt the voting outcome in their favour.

The monarchy in Morocco enjoys the full support of some Gulf states in this unholy war which is reflected in the division of OAU and the total indifference of Arab League to this issue. But in the wake of mounting world opinion, not even a single country has been able to side with Moroccan claim either in the UN or OAU. The Arab world is vertically divided over the issue primarily because of the money and muscle influence of some self-styled leaders of the Arab, African and Muslim world. Till early 1980s, Libya, along with Algeria, was supporting the Saharawi cause, thereby giving Pentagon a handle to chip in their arms and support. But ever since Libya has shifted its stance because of its internecine Arab politics. Washington has also distanced itself from a blatant pro-Moroccan position. But the most shocking aspect is the vacillating Indian stand in the matter.

India announced its recognition of SADR on October 1, 1985, accepting Polisario as the genuine liberation movement in Western Sahara and the right of Saharawi people for independence and self-determination. It had also maintained that there were no ties of territorial sovereignty between Western Sahara and Morocco which could affect the decolonisation of Sahara. But in last 10 years, Indian policy towards the fateful country has taken a somersault. There is an embassy for last 12 years. There has not been an ambassador for the last four years. Two proposals have been sent by Sahara for new ambassador but both have been lying in cold storage for the reasons best known to South Block.

Earlier Indian ambassador to Algeria was concurrently accredited to Sahara but for quite some time India didn't send an ambassador to Algiers. Finally when the charge of affairs was promoted as ambassador; Sahara was not included in his charge. Sahara has embassies in many countries such as Ethopia, Madagascar, Mozambique, Algeria and Angola in Africa, Venezuela, Cuba and Mexico in Latin America and Iran, apart from India in Asia. Except Mexico and India, there is a full-fledged ambassador in every country. Mexico has a promoted stand that it sends ambassador only on reciprocal basis. Since an embassy can't be opened in war-torn Sahara, it has also not sent one. But India has downgraded the status by not accepting the proposals.

We have cordial relations with Morocco despite its blow hot, blow cold atititude over Kashmir other Muslim issues in Organisation of Islamic Countries (OIC). It is the same OIC where an Indian guest delegation under the leadership of Fakhruddin Ali Ahmed was asked to leave the conference after a Pakistani protest. It is easily understandable that India doesn't want to offend the Arab lobby supporting the Moroccan position despite our age old stance against colonialism in Asia and Africa.

It was most surprising that the then Prime Minister Rao chose to visit Burkina Faso to open our embassy there in 1995, another Sahara baiter but refused to entertain a Saharan ambassador in New Delhi. Not that OIC has changed its stand on Kashmir after our distancing from Sahara or Morocco has come closer to us but the erstwhile champion of the third world seems to have lost its direction and thrust under the paranoia of imaginary fears.

An Analogy by Default: Korea and Kashmir

Korea and Kashmir were divided around the same point of history after the World War II, but the comparison stops there. The former was disunited by the superpower allies who redrew the world map to take revenge against the axis formed by Germany, Italy and Japan. But two statements made by two leaders in different contexts were tempting enough for an analogy.

President Kim Young Sam while celebrating the fourth anniversary of his presidency and the 78 anniversary of the March 1st independence movement, which paved the way for liberation of the then united Korea from Japanese domination, lamented at the sorry plight of the brethren in the northern part. On the other hand chief minister of Kashmir offered to part with Pakistan occupied Kashmir as a sop to peace. North and South Koreas are two entities which came into existence four decade ago because of the superpower rivalry while Kashmir was divided because of the fundamentalist designs of a newly born nation created at the altar of religious hatred.

One wonders why no one in India ever talks about the separated Kashmiris living on the other side of the international border or the Line of Actual Control whichever way you look at it. This columnist who spent a couple of days in PoK at the invitation of the then Bhutto government is painfully reminded at the horrendous conditions under which Kashmiris live there. The self-styled BJP nationalist leaders start hitting the ceiling at the mention of a prospective Kashmir solution. But has any one of them ever cared to know what is life like for a Kashmiri forcefully separated by a war and division?

President Kim's continuous efforts for a unification of two Koreas sound more authentic and genuine in direct contrast to the Indian crocodile tears. Ironically enough, defectors from North to South Korea, such as Hwang Jang-Yop, are still waiting in the South Korean embassy in Beijing for a reunion with the motherland.

Though it is not analogous to compare Kashmir with Korea by any stretch of imagination but there are many other comparable points such as corruption and graft in their body politic and society at large. The latest being the Hanbo scandal in which the president's son Hyun-Chul is being dragged without any apparent evidence. Kim had vowed to root out corruption in high places in the presidential election year. His resolve can't be dismissed easily as he has already brought two former presidents to the book.

His problems don't end there. All is not quiet among his ministerial colleagues who resigned en masse recently and the Korean workforce is vertically divided over his aborted labour laws for which he publicly apologized. As far as Hwang Jang-Yop's defection is concerned, he is confused whether to be happy at the development or take it with a pinch of salt as the process for peace with estranged northern brother is in progress. Last but not least is the mounting trade deficit despite his reforms and its fallout. All said and done, South Koreans in the fast lane of economic recovery. But understandably, their main concern remains the national security as the scars of alien domination and the division of the country are alive and painful.

As far Indo-Korean relations are concerned, they are on an upward swing with about 60 corporate giants rooting in the Indian market. People are talking about Japanese because of their imposing profile. It may turn out to be the proverbial hare and tortoise race. But with a small difference. In the last leg of this race, the Korean tortoise might be seen mounting a DCM-Daewoo Cielo or a Hyundai with Japanese hare on his Honda or Toyota far behind. Incidentally, some Japanese in India do share this perception.

India, Pak should Stop Playing Spy Catcher

India and Pakistan manage to find yet another spy in each other's capital every now and then declare them persona non-grata and pack them off. Both these countries have been playing this game of catching spies since independence. The very fact that as soon as one of them spots a diplomat indulging in undesirable activities, within 24 hours the other country manages to apprehend his counterpart again is sufficient proof that things are not as simple as they appear to be. Obviously, there is much more than what meets the eye.

There is a definite pattern which has emerged over the years in this diplomatic warfare. Whenever an Indian or a Pakistani prime minister is in a western capital like London or Washington, intelligence agencies start overworking to trap and frame one of the junior functionaries in the embassies of each other. It is evident that the message is more for global consumption rather than home constituencies.

Since the days of Chanakya after whom the diplomatic enclave in New Delhi is named wrote the monumental treatise in diplomacy called Arthshastra, the collection of information useful for the government back home is considered to be a bona fide activity of a diplomat posted at the host country. Now comes the question of the sensitivity of the information. If the relation between the host and the country to whom the diplomat belongs are cordial enough these activities are taken for granted. But if the two happen to be as hostile as India and Pakistan have been then even a sneeze becomes a storm. One still remembers the furore created at the innocuous visit of some Pakistani diplomats to Kerala. Though the visit was a routine affair, the local press there followed by the national press here made it out to be little short of espionage aimed at drafting Keralite Muslims against India. Little consideration was given to the fact that there is no love lost among Muslims in South India for Pakistan as they were not even considered good enough while envisaging the boundaries of Pakistan. Even the BJP admits that there is no comparison between the Muslim League of Kerala and the historical Muslim League of pre-partition India.

Ever since the contours of diplomacy have widened to include economic dimensions, conventional activities like propagation of an ideology or building of image has taken a backseat. Gone are the days when the then Soviet Union and other countries of the Europe used to spend a fortune churning out half a dozen bulletins to influence the Indian intelligentsia. Now even the USIS is drastically curtailed its budget because after the end of the cold war, there is no need for a competitive propaganda blitzkrieg. Now the brief of a New Delhi, bound diplomat is loud and clear. 'Assume the role of a hard core trader, sniff around to see what can be sold and purchased.' However, some die hard dogmatic regimes like Iran and Libya do care for the promotion of their ideologies and the image of their leaders but they are in a hopeless minority in the vast ocean of economic diplomacy which is here to stay ever since India set out on its programme of economic liberalisation.

In this context the insistence of Indian and Pakistan hawks to continue to play this spy game do not augur well in the changed scenario. Only recently even the Pakistani Prime Minister Benazir Bhutto told a Gulf news paper that the political differences can wait but let the business flourish in the true spirit of SAARC.

There have been very optimistic signs of prospective trade between India and Pakistan ever since businessmen from across the border participated in the SAARC trade fair when the divine voice of Nusrat Fateh Ali Khan enchanted the capital's' audience at Pragati Maidan. It is heartening to hear the desire from Pakistani, cricketers that India and Pakistan now play some tests at each other's home grounds.

That is the true spirit of modern diplomacy which can only be dictated by informal diplomats like artists, players, businessmen and journalists. It is evident that the intelligence - agencies have a job to perform but they are still governed by the age old diktats based on mutual suspicion and hatred. It must be replaced by the new concerns and realities. Unless that happens the strife torn subcontinent and the still staggering decade old SAARC movement cannot take off.

Who Divides the World into Haves and Have-Nots ?

Ever since I started reading newspapers I used to wonder why there was so much difference between my geography textbooks and the morning papers. There were long chapters on Africa, Oceania and the Sahara while the broadsheets were full of western Europe and America.

As I grew old, I was told that the world was not divided into seven continents and five oceans but the first, the second and the third worlds and that I belonged to the last with Asian, Latin American and African nations in tow. One fine morning, even the second world came to an end with the fall of the curtain in Moscow and its allies in eastern Europe. I was happy to note that I had graduated from the third to the second—little did I realise that the first meant the haves and the other the have-nots. Who made this division? I came to know the answer last week.

Sudanese ambassador in Delhi Awad el Karim Fadlalla invited Indian journalists to brief about the economic sanctions imposed "against her country which - obviously was in the second world—by the only custodian of the first world, namely the US. We have heard of similar sanctions against Iraq and Cuba but with little impact. The sanctions express unilateral arrogant outbrusts against poor countries who continue to be victims of the colonial past—British and Egypt in this particular case. It was a rare combination of an imperial alliance between a medieval and ancient super powers.

While imposing the sanctions, president William J Clinton decreed: "By the authority vested in me as president by the constitution and the laws of the United States of America included the international emergency economic powers I, William J Clinton, president of the United States of American, find that the policies and the actions of the government of Sudan including continued support for international terrorism; ongoing efforts to destabilise the neighbouring countries and prevalence of human rights violations including slavery and the denial of religious freedom, constitute an unusual and extraordinary threat to the national security and the foreign policy of the United States and hereby declare a national emergency to deal with the threat and order blockade of all properties and interests of Sudan in the US." Surprisingly, no one in the UN agreed with the US. Even in the US, 652 small and large businesses under the united name of USA Enagage reacted saying this action would only proliferate the unilateral economic sanctions as a primary tool of the US foreign policy. This would harm only the American business interests because other countries would continue to do business with Sudan, as is the case with Cuba and Iraq.

More than a dozen Indian journalists took copious notes of an hour-long explanation of host Fadlalla. The next morning I looked for some detailed analysis of the Sudanese predicament but to my dismay, I found none, thus belying the third world charge that the western media was singularly responsible in highlighting the issues pertaining to them. Here was a case when the third world media, which took great pains in grilling the ambassador about his laboured speech, had forgotten all about the issue by the time they reached their offices. I am not going into the details of the internal situation of Sudan. There could be a debate on the American sanction against this country but the fact of the matter is that Sudan is a friendly country which backed us in our bid to the Security Council elections last year and which has stood by us in the successive OIC (Organisation of Islamic Conference) summits. Thousands of Sudanese students including the warring factions of north and south Sudans are studying and fighting it out in Indian universities. India is even ignoring the expiry of their visas thus proving two points—firstly, India is friendly with Sudan and does not want to interfere in the internal affairs of that country, and secondly, it is democratic enough to allow free expression of conflicting views even on its home ground.

I was pleasantly surprised to see a large number of Urdu journalists in the Sudanese embassy on this occasion. More than Islamic solidarity, it reflected the presence of a foreign mission in Indian media rarely shown by its western and other counterparts.

I strongly feel that if 100-odd embassies in Delhi mean serious business with the Indian public opinion, they should divert their energies to the vernacular press which is decidedly influencing the Indian domestic policies. Therefore, there is no reason why they cannot tell popular

Indian preferences on humanitarian concerns such as the one created by the American sanctions against Sudan.

The afternoon ended with a sumptuous buffet laid out in the beautiful interior of the mission on the famous Shantipath of Chanakyapuri, which incidentally has been designed and built by Indian architects. According to press counsellor of Sudan Abdel Rehman Sharfi, the first African cultural centre in India would be opened soon in the premises of this embassy which might act as a nodal point for all the countries of the Black continent.

Latin Americans Stay Loyal Despite India's Faux Pas

If the crucial voting on Pakistan's human rights resolution on Kashmir had taken place this week, at least four Latin American countries would have voted for India.

Even minutes before Pakistan ate humble pie by virtually withdrawing the resolution, Brazil and Mexico took the floor to prevail upon Pakistan that it should not insist on voting.

It was not pure coincidence that our Latin American friends came to our rescue at the international forum. Since India's independence, they have never let us down.

The only exception is Ecuador who, for reasons best known to it, has always found itself standing alone against India.

In fact, the Latin American countries would have supported India despite a bureaucratic faux pas by South Block.

Chile, a staunch supporter of India in international fora and of late, very keen to heighten bilateral trade, was left out of a Kashmir-bound ambassadorial team by default. The team included the ambassadors of Mexico, Colombia and Venezuela, among other foreign envoys.

South Block realised its mistake only when the agitated Chilean ambassador demanded to know why he had been left out.

The team was suggested by none other than the new foreign secretary, K Srinivasan, and the head of the special cell created in Shastri Bhavan to counter the Pakistani offensive on Kashmir, VK Grover. It seems impossible that two such senior diplomats could have committed a faux pas of this dimension. Obviously, the slip took place when the file was shuttling between South Block and Shastri Bhavan.

Finally, when the then Chilean ambassador's complaint was looked into a ridiculous explanation was offered: There was no space in the plane going to Kashmir.

After this, if Chile had decided to abstain from voting in Geneva, we would have had no one but ourselves to blame.

South Block was also at a total loss to understand the singularly anti-India posture of Ecuador at Geneva.

Old timers point out that Ecuador did once have an embassy in New Delhi, which was closed down after dispensation in Quito gave shelter to Jagjit Singh Chauhan, the self-styled champion of the Khalistan movement. Chauhan later used Ecuador as a base for anti-India activities.

All this was recollected soon after Ecuador made public its intentions at Geneva. But none of it explains the Latin American country's animosity to India. It will not be sweeping to conclude that we are diplomatically insensitive to the Latin Americans, except on occasions like the recent one in Geneva.

Here is another example: Many things remain unexplained about why India was forced to postpone the much-touted G-15 summit, scheduled to be held in New Delhi last December. Everyone, including Prime Minister P V Narasimha Rao, was made to believe that the Latin Americans, who constitute almost a majority, let us down. But nothing is further from the truth, which is that we took them for granted and unilaterally postponed the summit from October-December to oblige a nearer friend, Malaysia, who was about to hold elections.

The Latin Americans returned the 'gesture' in the same coin. Fortunately, India was able to get its act together, and now, the G-15 summit is scheduled for the end of March.

At least 10 heads of state, including Carlos Menem of Argentina, have agreed to come. The latter is even keen to extend his stay for a bilateral visit.

This visit becomes more crucial for the G-15 because Argentina will be taking over as chairman from India. Argentina has occasionally cited the tardy progress made by G-15 to express its lack of enthusiasm for the movement.

Menem and Rao can sort out the future of this fledgeling body, provided India handles the Argentinian premier's visit with velvet gloves. So far it has not.

Presumably for security reasons, India has never been too keen to club bilateral visits with summits. At the time of the postponed summit last December, it had discouraged many heads of state who expressed their wish to do so.

This time, however, better counsel has prevailed, perhaps because of change of guard at the foreign secretary level. JN Dixit was known to be totally averse to the idea.

The Latin American argument is that it takes considerable effort to plan a visit to India because of the geographical mindset. Hence, if a head of state is in India, he would like to stay back and discuss bilateral matters as well. But till last heard, the file on Menem's visit was still stuck somewhere in the PMO.

Kabul Decides to Divide Hindus and Sikhs

It was to be expected sooner or later for 14 years, New Delhi backed puppet governments in Afghanistan and pursued policies which went against the natural aspirations of the Afghan people. Even when it was clear that the Mujahideen were all set to form the government, India in its in-herrent wisdom attempted to air-lift the ousted Afghan president Najibul-lah, gave shelter to his brother-in-law and Ambassador in Delhi, Ahmed Sarnav and made no efforts to gamer goodwill among the various fratricidal factions of the Mujahideen. As a result, Hindi films and songs were banned in Afghanistan, the Indian Embassy School was looted which resulted in its closure and thousands of Hindu families who have been living there for many generations have fled. However, one development was totally unexpected

Though there are about 40,000 Hindus and Sikhs in Afghanistan—mostly middle-class traders and shopkeepers, it is only the Hindus who are coming back. Even the Indian Embassy in Kabul is issuing road visas to Hindu families and under the excuse of 'proper scrutiny', is asking the Sikhs to wait. While the new rulers of Kabul are reassuring Sikhs in an attempt to make them stay back, they are also telling them to join forces with the Mujahideen to make its presence felt in Punjab across the Indo-Pak border.

These guerrilla forces, who were trained by Pakistan with the help of American arms in the prolonged war against the Russian-backed puppet government are still spirited—but without jobs. Now that they have the power, the Mujahideen government has decided to train its guns on India. The interim Afghan president S. Mojadeedi said in a recent interview to the video magazine *Eyewitness:* "Afghans feel a sense of betrayal on the pan of India for having supported an unrepresentative government in Kabul. On the other hand, we are grateful to Pakistan for the help throughout these years. Hence we are obliged to support their viewpoint, particularly with regards to Kashmir and anywhere else in the world for every just cause. "We strongly feel that Kashmiris should have the right of self-determination."

Coalition Governments are Here to Stay, World Over

Lok Sabha Speaker PA Sangma told a congregation of legislative presiding officers in Shimla that at least 60 countries in the world are being ruled by coalition governments. Though most of them are not experimenting with this phenomenon as is the case in India. But the Latin American region which consists of 33 sovereign nations ranging from Mexico in the US neighbourhood to Chile and Argentina at the confluence of Pacific and Atlantic Oceans have many similarities with the Indian scenario.

In terms of forms of government they can be broadly divided into two categories—the presidential and the parliamentary form of democracy. The latter largely comprising of the former British colonies in the Caribbean region follow the Indian pattern of choosing the leader of the majority party in parliament as the executive head of the state called the prime minister. These countries include Belize, Dominicia, Granada, Jamaica, Bermuda, Antigua, St Kitts, Aruba, Martineque, St Vincent, Anguilla, Trinidad, Tobaggo and Guyana.

Understandably, the number of political parties in the parliamentary system of governance is quite large compared to the presidential form of government. Thar is why, nowadays, a India-like coalition after elections is more evident in these countries. In direct contrast to this, direct election to presidency more often than not narrow down the number of contestants to two or three because larger the number, lesser the chances of winning. Thus, instead of a post-election coalition there have been successful attempts to forge pre-election alliances to avoid division of votes. The spectrum of political parties in parliamentary democracies is as wide ranging as in India. For example, in Nicaragua the 14-party alliance of The National Opposition Union of Violata Chamoro was even called the rainbow coalition in 1989.

The aborted system of power sharing by warring parties in Uttar Pradesh looked rather strange to Indians, but Latin Americans have known and practised it for the last four decades. For instance, the two main political parties in Colombia—the Conservatives and the Liberals—shared the presidency since 1957 to 1989 except for a break of four years in 1974. In 1989, after the assassination of liberal candidate Luis Carlos Galan, the new candidate—Cesar Gavaria—virtually achieved a landslide victory burying the sharing arrangement for good. But Colombia is unique in this regard and the success of this experiment for such a long time can be attributed to the menacing national problem of drug trafficking which it has been facing singularly in this region. This is the best example of how political parties—without entering into a coalition—have shared power for a common cause in the national interest. In fact, the Colombian politics revolves around narco-trafficking. Even the incumbent president Ernesto Samper Pizzano continues to face serious charges of poll funding by drug lords. If anti-drug virtually encompassed the whole region in the 1980s, the lurking shadow of the erstwhile military regimes vertically divided the political spectrum to contest for power. For example, the 17-party Concertacion de los Partido por la Democracia in Chile which supported presidential candidate Patriocio Aylwyn in 1989. This like the present ruling coalition in India, ranged from Christian democrat centrists to socialist leftists including even the ultra radicals. The basic difference between a pre-election alliance of a presidency to a post-election coalition of a parliamentary democracy does not end at reducing the vote division. It also speaks of the commitment made before the electorates during the campaign.

Such an experiment was tried on a national scale in India in 1977 when the Janata Party was formed. This experiment was shortlived because of the mechanisation of short-sighted and ambitious politicians. The experiment was possible because of the authoritarian Emergency rule suffered commonly by the opposition parties and leaders.

In Latin American also the concertacion of 17 parties came into existence in Chile to defeat general Pinochet's candidate Harnen Buchi in 1989. Similarly, the 14-party rainbow coalition of Violata Chamoro in Nicargua had its *raison de'etre* to dispose off Daniell Ortega of the Sandinista national Liberation Front.

Unlike India which gained Independence in 1947, freedom had started knocking the doors of Latin American countries in 1811 when Paraguay became free. But centuries of foreign rule gave way only to military dictatorships. This process remained for a century-and-a-half except for short phases of electoral democracy. Even these were plagued by queer systems, such as an elected president for life.

In Mexico's case the situation is even more incomprehensive where a single political party called the Partido Revolucion Ario Institutional (Institutional Revolution Party) has been in power since 1929 not as a result of periodical competitive elections but through a stage-managed, one-party domination where the same political outfit chooses successive presidents.

In the last two decades, a new democratic wave has been sweeping the Latin American region reinforcing the institution of regular multi-party electoral process in the region. Political parties which were not allowed a normal growth by the authoritarian rulers are entering into all kinds of coalition aimed at warding off the regional economic crisis as well as to keep the military in the barracks. Earlier, even if the elections were held they would either be annulled or the civilian governments overthrown by military juntas. Like it happened twice in a decade in Argentina—first in 1966 and then in 1976. Similarly, general Castello Branco staged a bloodless coup to overthrow Joao Goulart government in 1964 in Brazil. And it took exactly 21 years before a civilian government returned in that country. That is why political parties huddled together to cobble coalitions irrespective of ideologies or commitments they swore by. By and large, they were new parties because the people had rejected the traditional parties which were identified with the military dictators or had lost their appeal born out of popular pragmatism. Now there was no ideological plank but mere pragmatism. This scenario can be easily understood when compared to the present Indian situation where also traditional parties such as the Congress because of its monolithic semblance and the Bharatiya Janata Party because of the Hindu nationalism and suffocating discipline suffered loss in the 1996 general elections. The regional parties asserted themselves to stake their rightful claim in the national political pie.

Like Congress in India, traditional political parties in Latin America also drew their support from certain underprivileged sectors but ignored the larger social bases. Soon they found impossible to satisfy either. And the popular and well entrenched leaders had to make space for novices such as Fujimori in Peru. The newly elected leaders in Latin America have no particular ideological preferences because they have to keep their flocks together. They neither represent a particular vote bank of a mass base nor a social group.

Latin American experiments tell us that coalition governments are here to stay. Kennedy Simmonds has already led a coalition formation to victory thrice after 1981 in St Kitts, a Caribbean island known for different reasons in this country. From Ecuadore to Nicaragua, Latin Americans have successfully flirted with coalition partners and have shown that diagonally divergent parties mean more business than single party stable governments. The BJP which keeps harping on the advantages of a single party rule contradicts itself win confronted with the single leader find single party rules of successive Congress governments. There is only one example—of Mexico—where a single party has been in dominant position for the last 70 years. But, have we not heard the ills of Mexican economic fiasco?

India must Tread Cautiously in South Africa

India named the leader of its delegation to the swearing-in of Nelson Mandela in South Africa then Vice President KR Narayanan. The first option, however, was the President himself and later it was thought that the Prime Minister should head the delegation, as India has a lot at stake in South Africa, with 1.2 million people of Indian origin settled there.

Indians have always shown a natural skill for adaptation and survival particularly when it comes to alien powers. This is partly attributed to their tendency to align with foreign rulers at the cost of the local people, forgetting that one day the power would inevitably shift to local hands. It happened in Uganda, Tanzania and Kenya. It should not be surprising if it happens in South Africa as well, for Indians are in a precarious position there. The Natal province where they are concentrated, is a stronghold of the Zulu tribe. And the Zulus were virtually forced to exercise their franchise on the eve of last week's elections. Till then it was not certain whether Indians should be allowed to vole at all.

Even having voted now, Indians cannot derive any comfort because, contrary to expectations, the Inkatha Freedom Party of the Zulus have been unable to secure an impressive percentage of votes. Little wonder then that after winning a mandatory cabinet berth they have decided to sit in the opposition.

And whether Indians like it or not, their political fate is tied with the local tribesmen who have at no point of time dropped their demand for a separate homeland. And the Zulus are likely to pursue their demand more vigorously now than ever before, for it is not only their dream but a political necessity as well, for their very survival on the national scene. Or else, the African National Congress under Mandela's leadership is all set to swamp them in the black mainstream.

This is the darkest fallout of an otherwise all-colour elections. Ironically, Indians will find themselves at the centre of this gory chain of events which is sure to unfold in the days to come. Therefore India has to contain its feelings of camaraderie at this historic moment in Africa's journey to complete freedom. Clearly, the prospect of an eruption in Natal must temper India's thoughts on the euphoria in Pretoria.

Not that India has been entirely unable to decipher the writing on the wall. Both the tourism and civil aviation minister, Ghulam Nabi Azad and the minister of state for external affairs, Salman Khursheed, went to South Africa as the advance party for reconnaissance and spade work. They both came back with the impression that India should underplay its emotions.

They both dwelt on the historic role played by Indians in South Africa, from Mahatma Gandhi who won his political spurs there, to the part played by so many Indians in the struggle against apartheid. But when it came to talking of the role of the Indian community in the future—and the role of India itself to safeguard their interests—their voices were tinged not so much with emotion as with caution. And Khursheed was quite frank when he told Indians that they were South Africans first, second and last.

Fortunately, India has decided to deal with South Africans as a whole, and not with South African Indians only. The latter, India feels, would be adequately looked after by Mandela, who it seems will be fair in his handling of this influential minority.

While there may be cause to debate the role of the Indian community there in the anti-apartheid struggle, there cannot be any doubt about what India did to champion the cause of South Africa's oppressed black people, in international fora. It also cannot be forgotten that despite long historical and cultural links with that country, India refused to have any ties with the racist state. This effectively put paid to hopes of many Indian passport holders who wished to visit relatives in South Africa.

Indian passports will no longer declare that it is not valid for travel to South Africa, but the two countries will take a much longer time to change the approach towards the Indian settlers which has remained entrenched for the past century and a half.

India and South Africa are certainly destined to play a meaningful and construtive role in wider matters such as Third World affairs and North-South dialogues but both will have have contend with a kind of *laissez faire* when it comes to people of Indian origin. Otherwise the threat of yet another exodus cannot be ruled out.

Earlier, the Indians there could turn to the erstwhile rulers for help, but now that avenue is cut off, for the whites have a share of power under even the new system. They would not be inclined to come to the aide of a 'third force' because they do not need them now. The redeeming feature in this uncertain scenario is the support garnered by the National Party of FW de Klerk from people who are from non-white, non-black or mixed races. The latter group, which supported the racist regime, continues to the so for the same logic – to survive. It is obvious that they feel more secure under de Klerk's banner than the ANC, given their past actions.

Parliament Plays Diplomatic Host

Indian parliament hosted 500 odd parliamentarians from more than 100 countries to discuss how to increase share in political power in their respective countries and role in decision-making for six days. This six day exercise can easily be termed as the diplomacy of the highest order played to by the host, the then Lok Sabha speaker PA Sangma and Rajya Sabha Deputy chairperson Najma Heptullah. This is a sequel to the World Women's Conference held in Beijing a couple of years ago in which Indian governmental and non-governmental organisations participated in a big way. It has been possible because of the close cooperation between Indian Parliamentary Group and International Parliamentary Union a body older than the United Nations organisations. Incidentally, it was established in 1889 only a couple of months ago before Jawaharlal Nehru was born. But even after 108 years of its existence it has not been able to give the due place to women parliamentarians.

Barring a few exceptions women in politics owe their position either to the family lineage or by way of a compassionate consideration on account of being under privileged. Our 500 guests will be wrecking their brains for about a week on this very ticklish issue. It has been popularly put as how to increase the relationship between men and women in parliamentary democracies. On this occasion I am tempted to repeal questions like when will India have its first women President, Vice President, Speaker of Lok Sabha. Not that women haven't held important positions like governors, chief ministers, full secretaries in the so-called softer departments like education, culture, family planning but the point is why there is an obvious discrimination when it comes to the posting of vital significance.

Why go far, can America the biggest of the big democracies of the free world safely predict whether it will have a black President first or a woman? Before you jump to giving examples of Margaret Thatcher of Britan, Indira Gandhi of India, Sheikh Hasina Wajid of Bangladesh or even 50 odd lady ambassadors, can we conclude that the second sex as inaptly described by Simone de Bouevar has a proportionate share in all fora of decision making. If that was so, the on going Vigyan Bhavan conference would not have felt the need to discuss the issue like funding of women candidates in elections and training of women for political leadership.

Though the issues are global in nature they will be discussed on a regional basis among parliamentarians of Asia, the Arab world, Africa and Latin America. The problems of different regions are so divergent that it was felt necessary to discuss them even on a sub-regional basis. For example, today Sri Lanka, Nepal, Bangladesh, Malaysia, Indonesia. Thailand and the host India are meeting in the parliament house annexe to discuss the specific issue of women and decision making as part of the 13 sub-regional meeting held under the ageis of United Nations Development Programme (UNDP).

The main conference will be addressed by the then Namibian president Sam Nujoma, Bangladesh prime minister Wajid and former president of Iceland Vigdis Finnbogadittir. All this have been possible because of the pain-staking efforts by Najma Heptullah who thanks to her pioneering work in parliamentary democracy was elected to the executive committee of IPI and who according to the grapevine is likely to be elected as the vice-president in this conference.

Such conferences prove that diplomacy is not confined to bilateral visits signing of MoUs, cultural exchange programmes and cocktail circuits. Unless parliamentarians who represent the political will of their country confront global issues at multilateral fora, diplomacy will continue to be sweet nothings, 'cooperations' being only on papers. By hosting such conferences India has proved once and again that the individual and collective efforts of some of its leaders like Sangma and Heptullah go beyond the frontiers of this country. When 500 parliamentarians drawn from all over the world will be present in New Delhi at the opening of the budget session of Indian parliament they will see for themselves that not only democracy but the multi-party system which manifest the diversity of this country is alive and kicking.

Friends from Central Asia

The Central Asian Republics today are the most active group of countries in New Delhi. Though they arrived late on the diplomatic scene—after the dissolution of the Soviet Union—they are more convinced than India that there is a great potential of bringing bilateral relations on an even keel.

For them a national day celebration is not a routine affair like the one of Uzbekistan which I attended at Kamal Mahal in Maurya Sheraton. Their new ambassador Ithom T Nematov with only six months experience behind him, was bubbling with excitement at the turnout of distinguished guests which included Lt Governor of Delhi Tejendra Khanna (minus wife this time) and the recently defeated BJP sponsored vice-presidential candidate Surjit Singh Barnala. When we approached Khanna for exchanging pleasantries and expressed our desire to meet him for setting up a Latin American Centre in New Delhi, he was quick to response and gave us his fax number saying "Send me a line and I will meet you in the week after September 7". It was a pleasant surprise to see such professionalism from a high profile VIP.

Barnala was surrounded by sturdy Sikhs—I was told they all were doing business with Uzbekistan. It reminded me of an interesting bit of statistics that there is not a single country in the world which does not have an Sikh ntrepreneur.

Diplomats of all ranks from the Central Asian Republics were in full attendance to mark their solidarity with their brother ambassador Namatov, including the erstwhile Russian colleague Valerie L Vladinimorav head of the information department whose father, I was told, also held the same position in the sixties and seventies. At that time young Valerie used to be an engineer at 25 Barakhamba Road office of the information department. That historical building—at a stone's throw distance from Delhi Mid-Day's office—is being reconstructed. According to Valerie he was anxiously waiting for its completion so that he could regain the peace of his home at 2 Bhagwan Das Road which now houses his office as well. But according to the new 'apartment culture' of Delhi, the Bharakhamba Road complex is being designed into a high-rise building and the Russians will have only a part of it. It would be some change from the days of the Iron Curtain which used to segregate the diplomatic complexes from the rest of the society.

Central Asian diplomats seem to be sharing everything in life from housing complexes to jokes and even friends. It was a rare sight to be in the company of the ever-smiling Turkmein ambassador Ashir Ataev who was using the Kazak ambassador Rashid Ibraev and the Russian diplomat as an impromptu interpreter while cracking jokes with the guests. Being the first Central Asian ambassador that I interacted with I do have a soft corner for him. He informed me about the forthcoming visit of Prime Minister Gujral to his country about which they were very excited.

Kazak attach Yerkin has just recovered from a nasty appendicitis operation. So affected was he with anesthesia that he told me he came singing the Kazak national anthem in a delirium. He was not able to resist the feelings of a proud father. His wife Guinara has recently delivered a baby girl named Dinara whom he is yet to see, though the wife I am told dutifully dispatches the pictures of the baby who has just recovered.

One of the surprise guests included Dr Rikhy and his beautiful daughter-in-law who manages his Basant Lok hospital in the posh Vasant Vihar colony. They have rightfully earned the reputation of handling the traumatic cases including accidents and attempted suicides. Their emergency services are considered to be the best in the Capital, very diligently handled by junior Dr Rikhi. But that is not their only distinction—they are the most trusted hospital for the diplomats in Delhi after the British High Commission medical centre. They virtually monopolise the African diplomatic clientele. Dr Rikhi has really come a long way from his small clinic in Defence Colony: All because of his personal care for every patient.

It was a crowded evening for the ambassadors and other members of the circuit with Malaysian and Slovak receptions also being organised in the same neighbourhood. That is why the diplomats seemed to be making fleeting appearances like the Mexican who always comes up with a smart dress. But the description of the evening would be incomplete without mentioning the Egyptian lady ambassador Gilani Alam and Panamanian ambassador who was relieved to note that at least one Indian newspaper had mentioned the late

Egyptian millionaire Dodi Al Fayed's death in a major way who had died with Princess Diana in a tragic car accident.

Try Tashkent This Time, Instead of Mumbai

I met him at one of the diplomatic parties recently. Perhaps the Russian one to celebrate their national day and most probably the Turkmen ambassador Ashir Ataev had introduced him to me. He was looking a bit overwhelmed by the grandeur of a Russian do in the post-disintegration era. The same Russians who had presided over their destinies for long.

It was a brief meeting and I had forgotten about it. But a few days later, President's secretariat sent me a credential presentation picture and the image of the same suave and sophisticated ambassador came alive. He is the new ambassador of Uzbekistan Ilhom T Nematov.

He brings a rich repertoire of experience from Moscow to Germany. This is his first ambassadorial posting and he is full of enthusiasm about what he plans to do in India.

Soon he intends to bring out a colourful magazine on the eve of The 50th anniversary of Indian Independence. He would like to make films, produce coffee table books on Uzbekistan and organise cultural exchanges between the two countries. Talking about his country, he was proud to state that Uzbekistan

Airways is bringing planeloads of his countrymen and Indians employed in 57 joint ventures there every day.

The traffic is growing so fast that soon Indian airlines might start weekly flight to Tashkent. The aviation story of his country which has historical linkages with India since the days of Taimur Lung, his grandson Babur and the successive rulers of Mughal period as well as great historians such as Al Beruni of those times doesn't end with Delhi-Tashkent flights.

Uzbekistan airways has become quite popular with Indian tourists intending to go to Europe and even New York as they offer the cheapest ticket (Rs 14,000 to be precise to and fro London). He agreed with the contemporary historians such as Akhilesh Mittal that the so-called Mughal rulers of India were actually Uzbeks. He is also keen to see an end to the Afghan crisis so that something can be done about the mausoleum of Babur which is in disarray in Afghanistan.

Ambassador Nematov is determined to take our bilateral trade to dizzy heights which stand at US $ 42 today.

He finds a great potential for Indian entrepreneurs in the field of pharmaceutical, cotton and other infrastructure.

India has high stakes in Central Asian region because of its strategic position. These Republics could not interact with India on an equal footing because all the decisions were taken by Moscow. Not only the products manufactured were also centrally decided. For example, in case of Uzbekistan, which is the second largest grower of cotton, had to export 92 per cent of its produce.

If the same could be utilised for its domestic use in garment making, the economy would have been largely benefited. Today, Uzbekistan has been able to reduce the export to 72 per cent. The remaining is used in the domestics mills.

China, Korea and other countries in the region have fully realised the potential of this region. But Indian businessmen are still little sceptical.

It will be a great idea if Indian businessmen venture out in steel, hotel industry and hospital sectors and invest in Uzbekistan.

It is only two-and-a-half hour journey from Delhi. A little more than what it takes to reach Mumbai. Tashkent and other cities are historical places and have now been turned into modern centres for tourists as well as businessmen.

New ambassador desires that Indians at least visit his country once and decide for themselves.

4
Saying it Culturally

When a Pakistani Diplomat Plays Host

With over 100 diplomatic sessions in Delhi, the cocktail parties are a routine affair for the diplomatic circuit, but a private invitation from a Pakistan diplomat in his family ambience is something which creates curiosity and expectancy. Unfortunately, Indo-Pakistan relations never seem to see the light at the end of the tunnel. Thanks to political and intelligence warfare. Therefore, when I got such an invitation last week I was amused and anxious in the same breath. Amused at the prospect of breaking the monotony and expectation for the things in store for me. Contrary to popular perception there was no intelligence vigil to note down the who's who list of the guests at the gate. There were no ogling neighbours either. The entrance was wide open sans guard. Even the hosts were charmingly disarming. But not the guests who were fidgeting the whole evening in their seats, apprehending a quick turn which was nonexistent. It was a true reflection of our mindset about our neighbours.

I was a wee bit late to enter the house which was already full with assortment of guests drawn from diplomacy, media and business.

Contrary, to a western setting, it was a typical Indian drawing room where men and women were placed in separate corners and remained so for the entire evening. There were drinks but was served by Pakistani bearers with an element of devine guilt. The hosts obviously were nursing neat sodas through out the party but were at pains to make their guests comfortable.

The lady hostess in the true subcontinental mould had supervised every thing personally from cushion to cutlery and starters to dessert, and keeping in mind the ongoing Navratri she had taken extreme care to include some vegetable dishes for the guests. So far so good but the litmus test lied in the discussions to follow. Being a maiden exposure to such a setting. I was apprehending fireworks in tune with the skirmishes across the line of actual control. But nothing of the sort happened as the hosts very diplomatically brushed aside all attempts to draw them into a comment on Kashmir or Murtaza, leave apart Benazir or Deve Gowda. These taboos were conspicous by their absence even in the secluded conversations among foreign diplomats, Indian mediamen and functionaries of Amnesty. It remained a mystery as to who drew the dividing line, the diplomacy or discretion lest the host was embarrassed.

The house had nothing typical Pakistani either about its decor or artefact. In fact, it had a global touch reflecting the postings the hosts must have had before coming to Delhi.

Even the customary Islamic green and coincidental caligraphical 786 signifying the faith were missing.

Indians and Pakistani are drawn to each other through their music, serials and films. But the hosts made no effort to impose their culture on the expecting guests. The moral of the evening was loud and clear. Pakistani intelligentia including diplomats doesn't want to carry Indo-Pak relations on their sleeve every time. If there is any score to be settled, let it be done professionally in the concerned quarters, but in their day to dealings they want to treat us like any other country in the world, and it is purely incidental that once we were a part of the same geographical identity. That is history and period. Let's not be sentimental about it because the egg can't be unscrambled. It was reminiscent of a sub-continental post divorce scenario where two intelligent spouses don't want to be reminded of the good old days, as they have a present to live, and a future to look up to.

The bottomline was underlined by a carefully guarded reaction, that what happens in UP doesn't interest us as what happens in Karachi should not be your concern, but then Kashmir is a different matter.

Latino Ties and a Farewell

At The annual Christmas bash of the Venezuelan ambassador Jocelyn Henrique, a little bird cooed in my ears that her next station would be Beijing. She had been waiting for this news for quite some time now as she has already completed three years in New Delhi. India was her first posting as ambassador and its a rich tribute to her diplomatic acumen and negotiating skills that she has been graduated to China.

I can only say that India's loss is China's gain. I can safely presume that for all practical purposes it was her last Christmas in Delhi. That is why she had left no stone unturned to make it a memorable affair. The guest list included Secretary in the foreign affairs ministry, Lalit Mansingh, Joint Secretary for Latin America Homai Saha, ambassadors and high commissioners from Croatia, Somalia, Spain, Egypt and Trinidad and Tobago.

There was a fair sprinkling of journalists. Ambassador Jocelyn herself was looking elegant in a red slain shirt, keeping in tune with the Christmas festivities. The sumptuous table had everything one expects at a

Christmas feast, ranging from turkey to cheese and ham to cake.

Homai Saha was recently in Brazil, Argentina and Chile along with secretary Man Singh. It was a familiarisation trip for both. It augurs well for Indo-Latin American relations that both these functionaries are full of ideas and enthusiasm on further promoting bilateral and multilateral relations. Saha genuinely feels that everything will fall in place in the sphere of diplomacy. She reminded me that soon after Independence we used to think only in terms of Western Europe and America and no one talked about China and Japan. Then came a time when we entered into very fruitful and meaningful relations with them.

She is absolutely right when she says that economic and commercial relations are the bane in the area of promoting ties. For example, today Latin America is not taught in more than two or three universities even at the MA level. The reason being there is no market for the students passing out with this subject and there is no market because there is no substantial trade. There is no communication gap between us but there is definitely an information gap. This information gap cannot be filled by producing mere Spanish interpreters. We will have to upgrade the level of understanding and perception at a much higher level. This should not be a major problem because at least the present lot of Indian policy planners have started thinking in these terms and for this I would like to give a lot of credit to the present lot of Latin American ambassadors like our hostess of the evening, Jocelyn.

The earlier lot of envoys from that part of the world were concentrating more on art and culture, thus confining the relationship to the curiosity level and fulfilling the needs of the initiated segment of the intelligentsia on both sides. But the globalisation of the economy and the market forces have made it imperative for distant countries to speak the language of trade. The present lot of Latin American representatives, who have made high level visits possible in the last two years, have also created a need and a desire to talk business. Another interesting guest with whom I got another opportunity for a head-to-head talk was Mrs Ghosh of India International Centre. Both of us could not help broaching the comparison between IIC and its newly acquired neighbour, the India Habitat Centre. IIC has taken a serious note of IHC and it has made them aware that something will have to be done about changing the profile of IIC to keep in tune with the younger generation.

IIC is falling into the mould of IIC clone by organising exhibitions, plays, film shows, restaurant and bar sans the serious cerebral stuff. Meanwhile IIC is known for its role as a pressure group and think tank for foreign policy formulations. No one can deprive it of that image and IIC will have to carve out a niche for itself in its proclaimed area of environment and eco-friendly habitat.

IIC is still headless as its director NN Vohra is on call at the Prime Minister's in South Block. This has left the Centre in the hands of Kapila Vatsayan who has other priorities too. It is high time that IIC gets a new full time director to reorient its direction and the content of its programmes.

It's series on the Northeast has been received very well and for the first time in Delhi exposed its members to the remote corners of India. In short, one can conclude that an interesting competition is on the cards in the new year.

At last the rare combination of mundane financial bureaucracy and the vibrant Kathak dance, the enfant terrible Shovana Narayan, has brought her Austrian diplomat husband back home–this time in the avataar of the ambassador of his country. India is the country where the ambassador met his high profile wife, instantly fell in love and got married.

Shovana in Delhi and the diplomat husband globetrotting resulted only in cementing their relationship. His second posting in India has provided both of them a beautiful opportunity to mature it further. For the benefit of both of them, as individuals and the countries they belong to in general.

Trade can Wait, It's Culture Time

There could not have been a more opportune evening to celebrate the Chilean national day which fell on the eve of the first ever Davis Cup tie against India. With barely two months behind him in India, Benjamin Concha Gazmori told this columnist that he could not have had a better headstart. With a little luck on his side. Chilean president Eduardo Frei Ruiz-Tagle could pay the first ever visit by a Chilean head of state some time next year. Concha is in touch with the new director-general of Indian Consul for Cultural Relations Himachal Som to prepare a cultural backdrop for the probable presidential visit.

Aware of the little bilateral trade ($ 110 million) between the two countries and no miracle in sight because the Government of India is still keeping many fingers in the export pie and Chilean trade being totally in private hands, ambassador Concha wants to concentrate on the cultural front. According to him India is considered to be a land of ancient wisdom and civilisation and one which is deeply involved in the global affairs, therefore, it is a privilege to be posted here despite not being able to do much commercially. He intends to bring his national folkloric ballet as a sequel to the forthcoming tour of Odissi and Bharatnatyam classical dancer Sonal Mansingh.

Concha needs no introduction to Indian religiosity, theology and philosophy. His 24-year-old son Raul is camping at one of the *ashrams* in Jagannath Puri after being attracted towards Indian spiritualism, courtesy a guru he met in Chile. He has already visited India five times in search of an institution which could expose him to comparative religions. He even went as far as learning Sanskrit to quench his thirst for oriental knowledge. He was even willing to discontinue his four year degree course in theology at the internationally renowned institute of Freiburg where his father was posted before coming to India. Before getting attracted to religion, Raul was a like other teenagers enjoying all good things of life. But today, he is a teetotaler and a vegetarian creating problems for Iris Indian cook at the ambassador's house in Shanti Niketan.

It was surprising to know that Puri is becoming a popular destination for young Chileans in quest for higher moral values and a way of lifc quite different from the one which exists back home. That reminds me of former President Shankar Dayal Sharma's visit to Chile in 1995 where his traditional Indian attire of *churidar pajama,* black long coat and a Gandhi cap fascinated the Santiago citizens so much that they come out in large numbers whenever he went to public places. For them that dress code represented something pious and divine. Though there is very little interaction and a lot of ignorance about each other, the lure of culture is a permanent source of curiosity and attraction for Chileans about India. Concha wants to build on this curiosity.

He has no set agenda for his tenure because he feels that it is frustrating to set goals and not be able to achieve them. That is why he wants to take everything in the stride and go by the ear. He was impressed by Indian academic and popular interests in poets such as Pablo Neruda and Glabriela Mistral, the works of both having been translated into Hindi. The Spanish language centre of JNU is planning a special issue of their journal *Hispanic Horizon* on Chilean poetry under the editorship of Anil Dhingra.

Talking about the lawn tennis encounter between India and Chile at the Delhi Lawn Tennis courts, the ambassadors had predicted a 3-2 verdict in favour of India but also hoped for a miracle when though not unusual in Davis Cup matches where players vie for national honour rather than individual laurels, alas didn't come about. During his visit to Kolkata, he landed at a football stadium to witness a final match and came back impressed by the standard of Indian soccer. It was contrary to the popular perception that what football is to Latinos, cricket is to India. He sees no hope of an early introduction to cricket in his country where it is confined only to some Chileans of British origin. He did mention a national sport—called Rodeo—in which a calf is chased and brought to a fixed destination by players riding horses. He plans to introduce all such elements of Chile during his stint to fill the time space till commerce takes over.

Diplomacy of 'No-Coloured' People from Africa

Soon the imposing Sudanese embassy on Shantipath will have a cultural centre of its own. This will be the first ever cultural initiative by any African country in India. So far, this domain has been confined to larger countries like America, Britain, France, Russia, Israel and Iran. The new cultural centre will be a part of the chancery building, recently completed by the famous Khattar father-daughter team of architects.

They have already re-built the sprawling Iranian embassy on Barakhamba road and are now engaged in restructuring the erstwhile Soviet Information Centre on the same road. Africa has a very strong cultural content manifest through its folk arts, vigorous dance numbers and tribal artefacts.

During my two successive visits to Eastern African nations of Burkina Faso and Ghana and Zimbabwe and Namibia in Southern Africa with the then Prime Minister PV Narasimha Rao and President Shankar Dayal Sharma, I found that the great adaptability of African singers even to the Indian melodies of 1940s and 50s.

I vividly remember the moist eyes of Indian and African leaders when an African singer, after a couple of his local numbers, suddenly burst the atmosphere with a high voltage Indian film song. That evening was a pointer towards the potential of Indo-African cultural interaction and integration.

I am sure the prospective Sudanese cultural centre will eventually become the nerve centre of such a confluence of two cultures divergent in form, but convergent in content.

Sudan, the largest African country, is generally in news for reasons other than diplomacy. There are more than three thousand Sudanese students in India—one of the largest contingents of unofficial ambassador from its country. About hundred study in various institutions in Delhi.

A dozen of them being on scholarship under bilateral cultural exchange programme. They enjoy total freedom of expression to the extent of raising the voice of dissidence against their own political dispensation. Sudanese embassy is pretty cool about these activities despite its regimented image perpetuated by the Western media which continues to portray it in all dark shades.

Said Abdul Rehman Sharfi, first secretary in the embassy here, "our students have been getting Indian visa on a platter from Indian embassy in Khartoum because of the liberal policies pursued by India towards all African nations. Not all African students engaged themselves seriously in their academic persuits in India. Some get politicised. Others overstay and some even indulge in unlawful activities. But India has never allowed this to become a bone of contention with the concerned country. Of late, there have been evidences of some Europe-based human rights organisations funding and patronising student organisations from such third world countries whose political preferences do not fall in line with the western model. Sudan is one of them. Sudanese students are divided in as many groups as exist in the country back home and there have been cases of fierce arguments and at times minor violence after heated altercations. A small restaurant in the bylanes of the crowded Nizumudin is a case in point. Rival groups use its walls for their ongoing debate on political differences. Sudanese students throng to this restaurant for the latest arguments about the internal situation of the country.

Some students even use the columns of Indian media to air their grievances against their own government. Some even seek political asylum and consequent financial help from United Nations Commission on human right.

But Sudanese government has neither sought the deportation of any student nor tried to impound their passport. Its policy is to allow any lawful political activity even on a foreign soil because it believes in the basic human rights and dignity.

Sudan has more than 200 languages and 300 tribes which account for some of the ethnic tension in the country. Its people stand out among African community by its distinct colour which they prefer to call as no colour.

The official language is Arabic but most of them understand and use English. Sudan is one of those rare countries which supported India in its abortive bid to a non-permanent seat in Security Council and doesn't mince words in accepting it. It supports India on the issue of Kashmir even in a predominant anti-India

Organisation of Islamic countries. India needs to reciprocate African overtures like the forthcoming Sudanese cultural centre by reciprocating cultural exchanges and intensifying the exposure of Africa through ICCR which at times seems to be Eurocentric like our economic and political diplomacy. Some 3000-odd students from Sudan and its many more multiples from other African countries could well be used as a repository of Indian-hospitality turned into interactive diplomacy.

Egyptians in Delhi are furious that when London was flooding with tears for Diana, her late but not lamented companion Dodi was being quietly buried in a deserted cemetery. In the same breath they don't forget to mention that the Indian media was a little more kind to him.

The royalty couldn't comfort the disturbed soul of the princess who started as a nanny, a cook and then a kindergarten teacher before the dream prince arrived on horseback to woo her. That is why the palace and media couldn't reconcile to her indulgence with commoners like Khans and Dodis.

They treated Dodi equally, both in life and death. Dodi was no prince by birth, or marriage. That was why he and his father were denied citizenship time and again. But he was no less the inheritor of Harrods, the owner of hotels, yachts, aeroplanes and even islands.

Though much maligned, he was a man of taste. Had Diana fallen head over heels for a nobody? Would she have 'owned' him publicly if he was a lesser man? Many tried to bring solace and peace after the royal estrangement and separation but only Dodi took her on a roller coaster around the globe. No one knows whether they would have tied the nuptial knot.

Both had a bad marriage behind them. Both were being wooed by the glitterati but they were looking for something else. A heady mix of both worlds—

geographically and otherwise. Now it is for the French and their investigative skills to nail the real culprit. The paparazzi of both varieties, professional and commercial, were eager to know what chemistry was working.

One can heap millions of curses on the media curiosity, but were they only to blame. There are reasons to believe that even British intelligence was keeping a tab on their movements. Has it not been established that it was MI5 who photographed her with Major Hewitt in the proverbial bean haystack. All kinds of theories are in circulation. If the dead driver has been proved to have drunk a little too much, there are Kiwis who are claiming that the blood report could be wrong. Rumours are flying thick and fast, with even the high and mighty not being spared the accusing finger.

After all, what happened on the Mediterranean sea was no less than a national embarrassment. Agreed she had been divested of the royal inheritance but she would have been the mother of the king-to-be. Only the Iranian television had the misplaced courage to call Diana a moral disgrace of the British court who died in Paris but privately there would be many takers to this epitaph in various courts of the world. And all, this was on account of one man Dodi al Fayed who dared to tame the heart of the princess of the people, despite not being born with blue blood.

The clock turned full circle in less than a century when another royalty – King Edward VIII abdicated the throne to find solace in the company of a commoner widow Wallis Warfield Simpson. In that case also, the throne had fumed and fretted only to relent later to make him the Duke of Windsor and the governor of the Bahamas. Today he is better remembered than most of his peers.

Dodi could give Diana whatever she longed for in life except the crown. But although she had abdicated the latter in favour of personal freedom, royalty wanted that she be obliged that she was chosen to mother future kings. But she was cut out for bigger causes in addition to procreating future royal progenies.

She got married at 20. By 23 she had delivered the prince to the royal throne. After that she wanted to play a bigger role as a champion of international issues like landmines and aides but somewhere it clashed with the ego of others in the family. They saw her image being taller than all of them put together. British royalty is known for their charities but that was more on account of the throne than their personal charisma. Here was an outsider who came from the cold and stole the thunder. The ensuing clash ended in personal landmines. First they settled scores within the wedlock and later out of it.

Even the divorce didn't deter her spirits. While she was coining to terms with her personal trauma, the mother of all tragedies struck her. What she was trying to do could not have left the royalty in peace. Everyday headlines were giving them sleepless nights. The prince could not match with her profile despite being the heir to the throne. He seemed to be a pale shadow of his former wife, who proved to be better half more after the separation.

At such a juncture the news of her sudden disappearance from the scene was more than a bolt from the blue. The first reaction was probably of shock, replaced by dawning reality and the third was to make best out of it. Initially they joined the chorus of the media but soon took the charge. Diana died in a crash, also the man who was accompanying her for last one month, after that the reference stopped.

Then came the witchhunt. The car was going at more than the desirable speed. The driver was more drunk than permissible. The prince will bring the body but she will not get the state funeral. Heads of state were not expected. Only distinguished citizens will be invited. Meanwhile

Dodi was buried unheard, unsung, but for the popular upsurge even she might have been buried incogniton.

Last word: More than two millennia ago, European emperor Ceaser crossed the Mediterranean to win the land and heart of an Egyptian queen, Cleopatra. He came, he saw and he conquered all he surveyed. An Egyptian commoner reversed the Ceaserian track to win the heart of a European princess. He also came, saw and won all but alas the story ended abruptly. Maybe history will be kinder to Di and Dodi.

Sports and Diplomacy

It may sound strange but it is true that the eight sports complexes set up and run by Delhi Development Authority (DDA) have contributed a lot in promoting India's bilateral relations, by providing playing and coaching facilities in various sports disciplines. The Saket sports complex under the dynamic leadership of Colonel OP Maheshwari is a case in point.

Saket is not a diplomatic area but gone are the days when embassies and diplomatic residences were confined to Chanakyapuri. As many as 23 diplomats and about half a dozen embassies are put up in and around Saket. Most of them use this sports complex either as full members or as guests of Indian members. Ever since the golf driving range off Aurobindo Marg started functioning, it has become the latest hub of diplomatic interaction with Delhi-ites. This golf course which has fulfilled the long-awaited golfing needs of South Delhi is going to be the latest craze in the days to come.

In fact, sports is one area which has contributed in making the life of the diplomatic community more enjoyable. There are regular tennis tournaments organised under the aegis of Group 4 security services at Hyatt Regency Hotel, which have attracted ambassadors and their families. The Somalian ambassador, who is a regular at the daily sessions and the occasional tournaments feel sporting facilities are better than most of the other areas in the Capital. The Delhi Lawn Tennis Association courts on Africa Avenue has got excellent coaching facilities. One of the notable coaches is Gajendra Singh who has earned name and kudos from the diplomatic fraternity. Recently he was the Indian representative to the Chilean Davis Cup squad who had come here to play against India.

Coming back to Maheshwari's sports complex, its virtual round the clock activity, especially the tennis courts has become a buzzword not only for diplomats but even for the expatriate community like Koreans who reside in the adjoining Sainik Farms. Despite all the adverse publicity, these farmhouses have the privilege of hosting Bangladesh High Commissioner and many African envoys as its inmates. In Saket itself, we have the Chilean second secretary, in Panchsheel Park there is the Venezuelan embassy, Cuban ambassador's residence, Trinadadian High Commissioner's residence and the Cambodian embassy. Though these diplomats have contributed in shooting the rentals, it has added to the quality of neighbourhood life also. One may say anything about the quality of DDA constructions but when it comes to sports, this organisation has done wonders. And not all of them are losing prepositions. One of them claims to have a timed deposit of Rs 64 lakh.

Delhi doesn't have much of a sports culture. It has not produced many players even of national fame, forget talk of international standards. But of late, at least two sports—tennis and golf—have caught the fancy of not only the higher strata but even the much maligned middle class. For that, the international companies have come up with generous sponsorships. The Saket sports complex has successfully introduced the team championships in addition to the individual honours. Catching them young might be a popular phrase but involving schools as institutions is a novel idea and has done wonders.

The Indian position and performance in the international arena has been dismal, the main reason being the highhandedness and politicking of sports federations. This hegemony needs to be replaced by public and corporate participation. DDA through its complex has shown how. What is needed is the sporting environment in encouraging school-going kids to come to the field and courts. It is an astonishing sight to spot boys under six hitting tennis balls against the wall at Saket complex. It belies the myth that the so-called western games are cost-oriented and therefore unwieldy. Nothing can be further from the truth. Only seeing is believing. And finally the sporting interaction between Indians and foreign guests make that possible which many rounds of hard negotiations may not.

Forging Cultural Linkages

The Debàte between ethnicity and nationalism is far from over. Though in the Indian context, it is confined to half a dozen countries including Fiji, Guyana, Surinam, Trinidad Tobago and Mauritius where there is a large presence of the people of Indian origin who had left the motherland a century or more ago. In some cases such as Mauritius and Fiji, they have retained the colloquial flavour of various dialects like Bhojpuri and still observe most of the religious festivals and social customs which they had taken in their cultural baggage when they left for greener pastures.

But across the Atlantic, most of them have forgotten the language. Many of them do not even remember what was their fatherland like. Not that they have completely submerged their identity in the new milieu, they are Indians only for historical records. Should a serious attempt be made to bring these people back to their roots.

This question came alive at a reception organised by Bharatiya Bhasha Sammelan (Council of Indian Languages) of Ved Pratap Vaidik in his modest but ambitious outfit at South Extension some time ago.

The occasion was the visit of two Gosain brothers—Prem Narayan and Shyam—who had come from Trinidad & Tobago with their families on a pilgrimage-cum-exploratory trip. The two Gosains are engaged in the propagation of Hindi language in their twin island country which has about 30 per cent Hindus and Muslims whose forefathers had gone as indentured labourers to work in the British owned sugarcane fields 150 years ago. They run an organisation called Hindi Nidhi (Hindi trust) which hosted the world Hindi conference last year in Port of Spain.

The proceedings at the reception were conducted in Hindi where speaker after speaker including Baleshwar Aggarwal, Lallan Prasad Vyas and many others spoke about the need to teach Hindi to those who have forgotten their mothertongue and to revive interest in religious works such as *Ramcharitmanas* and *Bhagwat Gita.*

The host and the founder of Indian language council as well as an institute for foreign policy formulation called *Bhartiya Videsh Niti Sansthan* even said that whenever and where ever the people of Indian origin were in crisis, Indians back home should stand up in their defence and support.

Vaidik is not alone in this pursuit. There is a considerable lobby in this country which feels that it is incumbent on India and Indians to protect the political and cultural interests of the people of Indian origin though they might be foreign nationals of a sovereign country like Trinidad and Tobago. This is a serious matter and has landed South Block in diplomatic soups in Fiji, Surinam and even Guyana. One cannot doubt the nobel intentions of Vaidik and his colleagues in their desire to consolidate the cultural linkages amongst Indian diaspora but a basic line has to be drawn between the responsibilities of a foreign national of an independent country and his ethnic aspirations.

In most of these countries, different denominations of a dialect called Creol have developed which is the connecting like amongst Indians with Africans, Europeans and the indigenous peoples. I don't agree with Lallan Prasad Vyas when he says that since Creol has a negro base, it is an inferior dialect and people of Indian origin should be encouraged and helped in replacing it by the modern Hindi as spoken and written in India today.

The dialect which the people of Indian origin had taken with them in the last century is not spoken here any more. The noted linguist Peggy Mohan has done extensive research on this subject and has come out with startling revelations that Indian Trinidadians have retained the original flavour of Bhojpuri which has been totally corrupted by the passage of time in India. R Narayanan, professor in Jawaharlal Nehru University's Latin American programme was also similarly amazed when he heard an old lady speaking to him in chaste Tamil during his visit to Port of Spain. When someone from the audience suggested to the visiting Trinidadian prime minister Basdeo Pandey at the India International Centre last year as to why doesn't he import some of the original Indian culture, he shot back that he was told that Indian culture was purer in Trinidad than found in India. The argument is very simple. You can't and shouldn't try to take the clock back and impose a linguistic excess baggage on the people of Indian origin only because their forefathers lived here.

You don't need to know modern Hindi to understand and appreciate *Ramcharitmanas.* There are better ways to forge cultural linkages. Some clues were given by the visiting Indian Trinidadians themselves. An Indian like any other foreigner has to stand in a queue before our high commission for a visa stamp. Why can't his passport be stamped on his arrival in India at the airport? If some of them want a dual citizenship why the option can't be offered the way China has done in case of its diaspora. According to Ashok Srivastava of the Indian Council for Social Science Research (ICSSR), Hindus of Trinidad are more traditional and original in their observance of the rituals and festivals. I experienced the same during my four-day stay in Trinidad a couple of years ago. But they find it difficult to get the ingredients required for fasting, feasting and festivities. Indians can provide that. Many of them want to visit Banaras, Haridwar and Kurukshetra but do we make their journeys memorable and pleasant?

Of Diplomatic Parties and National Days

It's party time in Delhi these days. The generous hosts are looking for occasions other than national clays to treat their guests with the best of cuisine and matching ambience. More than hundred Chinese companies spread their wares at the Pragati Maidan in the first ever Chinese Commodity fair. I was surprised to be amidst five hundred odd modern Chinese gathered at the Jaracanda Hall of the newly launched India Habitat Centre to celebrate the fair. Sharing the table with a metal and mineral exporter from Beijing, I came to know that the most delicious dish in their cuisine continues to be snake which sells at $ 100 a kg because it is not readily available in the weather of north China. Noticing a strange shock on my face, my fellow guest from the land of the Great Wall was prompt in revealing that finding elephant and cow together on the same road in Delhi was most astonishing to him. He had not seen such a sight anywhere in the world. And since he had seen more of the world, I had to believe him. The other sight seen by our valued guest was women carrying piles of bricks on their head. He was pleased to see a Chinese restaurant at every nook and corner of Delhi but was not exactly satisfied with their quality and taste of their cuisine. He said that Americans have been able to copy the Chinese food to the tea. No wonders they are doing a *tango se.* perfectly!

The other remarkable event of the week was the Rogelio Sinan award function of the Panamian embassy in India. Sinan, apart from being a poet and prolific prose writer from a small country in Central America was his country's consul in Kolkata in the 1930s.

Central America according to Prof R Narayanan of the JNU has torn itself as under by letting the Panama Canal flow through its territory. Sinan's brief sojoun in Kolkata impressed him so much that he wrote many of his poems and prose on that city in particular and the country in general.

Panamaian ambassador Mirta Saavedra Polo earned kudos that evening from none other than Kiran Bedi, Shivani Vazir and the unforgettable Lok Sabha, PA Sangma for charting out unconventional courses for promoting ties between the two countries. She doesn't celebrate her national days by throwing cocktail bashes but by visiting Tihar jail and orphanages to bless the have-nots with blankets and pullovers.

December happens to be the month of maximum national days. I have already attended the Kenyan and Japanese while the Bhutanese is on the cards. So are the annual thanksgiving reception by UN information director Feodor Starcevic and the Xmas eve of Jocelyn Henrique, King of Venezuela.

Something which stuck me most about the Kenyan party was the presence of ministers, counsellors and secretaries of various embassies having close relations with that country. Generally such functions are attended by ambassadors and high commissioners but Kenya recorded a rare gesture by insisting on Number Twos' and Threes' presence. Sharif of Sudan and Gokul Singh of Mauritius were at their charming best while making their presence felt through their national attires and concerns such as the Indian Ocean Rim Association for Regional Cooperation.

Ever since Prime Minister Gujral has placed his friend Krishan Kant in the Vice-Presidential chair he seems to be representing the former by being the chief guest at all diplomatic function these days. It has suddenly raised the level of these traditional occasions.

Before signing off I would like to mention the tempura stall put up and personally supervised by the Japanese ambassador last evening at his residence. The long queue at the stall reminded of *pakora* and *kabab* corners. Shrimps were being deep fried and offered to a galaxy of dignitaries waiting in the queue. But later on my father who is well conversant with the Japanese language and its traditions told me that tempura serving is not complete unless served with a dish of *saake* which is a rare combination of beer wine and sea food.

While coming out of the Japanese reception I spotted Charat Ram of DCM. Desiring to pick up a small talk with the veteran Delhiwala, I asked him about Indo-Japanese relations and the discourse which he gave on the Indian media and its futile questions and reporting made me think about the widening gap between the old and the new generations about the role of media and what people of yesteryears feel about the growing colour and glamour of print media.

But the most interesting event was when Toshiba general manager and Japan Airlines (JAL) boss, both Japanese spoke, to me in chaste Urdu and Japanese.

Time for Independence Celebrations

Barely had the flood of farewell parties for the Chilean ambassador Uldaricio ended when the frenzy for the 50th year of Indian Independence to be celebrated by the African missions in New Delhi began. At the Yemen national day celebrations, African ambassadors and high commissioners huddled together at the corners of Kamal Mahal in Maurya Sheraton, plannng over the scotch glasses the events to be unfolded.

The events included a seminar, a marathon in the early hours of one summer day ending with a sumptuous breakfast at the South African high commissioner Jerry Matsila's residence and Africa clay (night in this case) party at the Ethiopian ambassador's residence. Ethiopia coincided it with the foundation day of Organisation of African Unity (OAU), it being the current chairman.

African food, cooked jointly by the diplomats' wives was served endlessly at the party. The ladies, dressed in floral headgear, saw to the serving of the exquisite dishes themselves which gave the real flavour of the commitment, much to the delight of the guests. And hardly any one bothered about the sudden warm evening which added a little irritating note to the party. The most conspicuous was the absence of the Moroccans who chose to stay away from these celebrations as they are out of OAU for their dogged stand against Western Sahara.

It won't be out of the place to say that a diplomatic mission in New Delhi is known by the style in which it throws its parties. In this week's column, I take my readers to the Russian diplomatic world, which is different not because of its sheer size but the personal touch they give to it, even after the disintegration of the Soviet Union.

The Russian diplomatic complex in Chanakyapuri is the single largest compared to any part of the world. They have more than 100 diplomats posted in New Delhi and in other metropolitan towns of India and a dozen-odd sprawling offices and housing complexes in Chanakayapuri and Vasant Vihar and other parts of the Capital. Even after formal separation, Russians have accommodated diplomats including ambassadors and their families from the breakaway CIS countries in these complexes.

Most of the Russian parties are hosted in the common rooms of these residential blocks. Today, it may be perhaps on account of the economy factor. But even in yesteryears when vodka used to flow like Volga, these parties had the same character. An improptu bar is set up. The male members double up as cooks to lend the personal touch to the culinary. By now, the regulars at these parties can describe the various degrees of pungency in marinated cucumber.

Russians are integral part of the various diplomatic groups like the one on disarmament who host select and periodical gatherings of those dozen countries who share common concern over the nuclear proliferation in the world.

Despite the ongoing honeymoon with the West, Russians have not wavered a bit in their traditional ties with India. These days it is more than evident in frequent parties thrown by them where Indian and Pakistani diplomats posted in New Delhi can be seen locked in animated discussions over the future of Afghanistan.

They don't miss the single opportunity to attend such parties, first to justify their position in the present Afghan imbroglio and secondly to see if Indo-Russian nexus still exists. The imposing Russian housing complex at Nyaya Marg is a self-contained world. There are department and separate drug stores, their own Russian school and the famous Russian community which I was told lies somewhere between sauna and Jacuzzi.

Gone are the days when the medium of Russian interaction used to be their own language. Today, they learn English and other *lingua franca.*

And guess who is tracing them in English. None else than the newly-acquired friend, philosopher and guide—the US.

Whatever verdict history may deliver for Gorbachev, Russian diplomats don't mince words while pulling the entire responsibility for their miseries at his doorstep. Feeling that though his intentions were noble, his execution of it was shortsighted and clumsy.

But they say all this not with any rancour. In fact, Russians have learnt fast to laugh at themselves.

Happy Union!

Until I was invited by the cultural department of the Chinese embassy, I had not realised how big a drama was unfolding in the southeast Asian theatre of contemporary history.

It was a diplomatic party thrown by the Chinese to celebrate and announce that return of Hong Kong, after a century and half, was eminent. They also screened an hour long film before the usual clinking of scotch glasses and exchange of visiting cards in the well lit reception area of the sprawling complex of the embassy in Chanakyapuri.

The reception area had been done up with rare photographs and an interesting article on Hong Kong. When I requested for a copy of the article, I was informed that a Chinese staffer would help me get a photostat copy. As I requested the staffer (a somewhat old gentleman), he asked if I could speak Hindi for he could barely understand English. Then in very chaste Hindi he asked, *"apko woh vivaran chahiye?"* and disappeared somewhere behind those elaborate Chinese paintings hung on corridor walls to get the same.

I do not know-how many diplomats and Indian guests went back impressed by the painstaking efforts of the Chinese to tell the world that every Hong Kong citizen was happy with the prospects of what they had chosen to call as Hong Kong.

There were many interviews in the film. One of them which caught my instant attention was with a Hong Kong businessman of Indian kingpin by the name of Shikari. He like impeccable Chinese like any other native, courtesy his third generation lineage in the island country. Through his larger than life visage. Shikari was frying to impress his audience. It was relayed to us through commentators and translations that they did not fear the Chinese takeover. One cannot miss the emphasis which the Chinese are laying on the retention of capitalist system in an otherwise Marxist nation. The Chinese are aware that the whole world is watching with apprehension rather than curiosity how well Hong Kong integrates with the mainland.

The Chinese had carefully chosen the guests for the evening as most in the party had a Hong Kong connection—Umesh Gupta, the assistant vice-president of Gammon whose company had laid some vital infrastructure; Vineet Kumar, an artist with the Garhi complex: PL Verma, a rural culture protagonist Josiphina Villamere, a Filipino as well as Alexis E Scott Zko, the American second secretary have all been familiar with Hong Kong.

Though more than three-fourth of Hong Kong settlers are from China. Indians also have a significant presence in this island country. These Indian businessmen have deep rooted connection with their counterparts in Mumbai. United Airlines has already connected Delhi with Hong Kong. With this headstart, it will be prudent for Indian diplomacy, in business, to take some bold and broad initiatives to claim a big slice in the Hong Kong pie.

Another big do of the week was the Russian national day celebrations. The celebrations were held in the premises of the Russian, embassy which is not far from the Chinese embassy. It was a big affair with the far from the Chinese embassy. It was a big affair with the front runner presidential nominee, KR Narayanan as the chief guest. It was quite embarrassing for the Vice-President to receive congratulations, ahead of elections, from all and sundry. But the diplomat in Narayanan didn't let him betray his discomfort.

Russian may have have defected to the western camp but the world still considers them a power to be reckoned with. This was evident from the full attendance of the diplomatic corps—from Finland to Spain to Cuba to the new arrival from Uzbekistan.

The chief guest was seen sharing a 'secret' or two with the Egyptian ambassador, Gillane Allm. In fact, this self-effacing woman envoy keeps a low profile—in contrast to the awe she inspires on account of her deep knowledge on West Asia, in particular, and global issues in general. Some of the rare appearances were editor-turned full time BJP functionary, KR Malkani who confided to a colleague that the BJP might not have any objection to KR Narayanan being as the next President and Najma Heptullah as his deputy. How correct was he who said Indian polity was maturing!

Another surprise guest was the second son of Lal Bahadur Shastri, Anil who has travelled a long distance from Voltas to a management school via ministerial politics, courtesy VP Singh. We did talk about his elder brother Huri Bhai though we did not know that he would not be amidst us soon enough. After a long time I met a seasoned diplomat. Vinod Grover who almost missed foreign secretary's job because Gujral had opted for an extension to Salman Haider. Each time I run into the Cuban ambassador Olga in a parly I find her more charming than ever. The way she was sportingly negotiating compliments reminded me of the old world charm. Olga is busy as ever with an unending stream of delegations from her country.

I rounded off the evening in the company of two Hindi stalwarts Rajendra Awasthi of *Kadambini* fame and Ganga Prasad Vimal. Both of them have contributed immensely through their translations and travelogues about the world around us. But the sweepstake belonged to our old friend Ramesh Bhatia of Vasant Continental who always has an invitation for next evening in his pocket.

Of Venezuelan Fuel, Mansingh and Caricatures

The ambassador of Venezuela Joeleyn Henrique King organised a reception in honour of her country's external relations minister Miguel Angel Varelli Rivans who was in India last week to discuss Indo-Venezuelan relations.

I was glad to see Jose Clavijo, head of Asia in the Venezuelan ministry and the former *charge de affairs,* Venezuelan embassy in India among the Venezuelan delegation.

I still remember fondly the breakfast me and my husband shared with Jose and his newly married Dutch wife at the Taj Mansingh.

I also remember the moment when they watched to their horror my little five-year-old son devouring a plate full of plain butter as if it were the most delicious food in the world.

That was just the day before they were leaving for Venezuela. Time takes strides, and so much has changed in our lives!

Among the delegates were prominent businessmen hoping to sell, 'orimulsion,' an alternative fuel considered to be cheaper than traditional varieties.

The plus point of orimulsion is its 30 per cent water base, making it safe. Both the minister and the head of the organisation producing orimulsion were at their eloquent best, handling probing questions from a battery of select journalists invited by the ambassador at her Prithviraj Road residence.

This place is one of the best locations in town, and is at a stone's throw distance both from the greenest spot, Lodhi Garden and the most exotic shopping joint, the Khan market.

Next day the house was the venue of a reception for the minister. As usual, it attracted the best of diplomacy as well the social circles of Delhi. Much in demand was Lalit Mansingh, the safest bet for the next foreign secretary's job.

Though he coyly patted the mention at the prospect but was more than enthusiastic to discuss anything else under the sky, as far as Indian diplomacy was concerned. Given the present lot, he seems to be the obvious choice. But then South Block is never predictable in such matters.

The chief guest, Rivans had something to say about every prominent Indian he had met in last 24 hours. He found Prime Minister Deve Gowda as the wise man of India who seemed to know every thing but spoke precious little. According to him, Finance Minister Chidamabaram has all the intelligent questions in his kitty and Commerce Minister Ramayya, who recently visited Brazil was very affable and courteous.

The last I heard at the party was that the ONGC officials were still racking their brains, about the cost effectiveness of orimulsion as compared to fuel purchased from Nafta.

The Venezuelan ambassador is one of the most active envoys and a super hostess. Just last month, she had hosted a dinner for Niranjan Desai, our ambassador designate for Venezuela, taking care to invite all his personal friends, and a good number of diplomats and her friends.

While she pulled me aside before dinner to see her exotically set table "what do you think of it," she asked. "Doesn't it look tropical?" Indeed it did, the only thing which was missing was punacolada, which of course couldn't be served even during the fag end of the winters.

I looked at the different varieties of cheese spread on the table. "When there is a variety of cheese on the dining table, I forget everything else and just head for the cheese," said the Chilean ambassador smiling all the while and taking a second helping.

I bet he must have played an extra game of tennis or squash, whatever he plays to keep himself so fit and trim.

Another important event of the week was the Ghanian national day on the sprawling green of the high commission. There was cause of double celebration this time.

Apart from the national celebrations now they have a man in the UN headquarters as the most important functionary of the world today.

The last incumbent also from Africa challenged the might of the empire, but Kofi Annan is known for his re-conciliatory approach, than confrontatist posture. Like any other African congregation, this one also brought out different diplomats in their colourful traditional attires. The accompanying music made every foot tap.

The week rounded off with a splash of colour in the true spirit of the approaching Holi festival.

The venue was AIFACS art gallery and the occasion was the indomitable Rakesh Sehgal who seems to have converted the journalistic caricaturing into an art, catching the mood and spirit of any city he is invited to.

'Rakesh has a knack of catching the mundane, with a fascinating angle. After seeing his 30 odd paintings on different aspects of Korean life, one came back with a feeling that he was an expert on the city which seemed to have every thing on the road; from dancing girls to musical concerts; from restaurants to wild animals.

With every new exhibition, Sehgal is maturing in his captions which are full of jibes and not always on others.

But the best came from his young wife who had remarked on the introductory remarks on the artist as a husband.

The handsome brochure read, "he is not only a cartoonist but he is a cartoon himself!"

Panama Picks up Indian Ambassadors of Mania

First it was the Argentina embassy, then the Cuban embassy and now the Panamian embassy in India will be rewarding the Indian winners of an essay competition on Panamanian poet Rogelio Sinan on December 10 at FICCI's Federation House auditorium. And whom have they invited to distribute the awards? Lo and behold. Lal it Mansingh, the ebullient dean of the Indian Foreign Service Institute which trains Indian and foreign diplomats at Akbar Bhavan round the year. Why? Because by generating interest and awareness in a far-flung country like Panama, its ambassador is doing nothing but preparing Indian ambassadors for the years to come.

Diplomacy has many faces. It's the art of influencing people and winning friends in an alien land. Some choose age-old methods like signing MoUs, organising bilateral visits and holding national day celebrations. Latin Americans, known for their cross-cultural personalities tend to choose altogether different ways.

The Cuban ambassador requested a Sarvodaya school in RK Puram to rename itself after the legendary revolutionary Jose Marti. The Colombian ambassador hosted a joint Latin American thanksgiving party on her spacious lawns at 8, Kautilya Marg on the eve of last Christmas and the Mexican counterpart hosted a poetry recitation evening at his bare-brick bungalow on Prithviraj Road where the charming compere Arshiya Sethi stole the limelight through her effervescent voice.

But Panamanian ambassador Mirta S Polo, whom I met a couple of years ago at a diplomatic party has been distributing layettes to the newly born babies at Kalavati and Kasturba hospitals to mark her National Day every year on November 3. She also donated 180 bedsheets to an orphanage run by the Missionaries of Charity and gave a cheque as donation to Kiran Bedi's India Vision Foundation. What's more she is so impressed by the Jaipuri foot for the disabled that she is sending a representative to her country to train technicians. This cannot be dismissed as stray charity work. Its simply a thought, a gesture as feeling for the people of this country. The Panamanian poet Rogelio Sinan on whose memory the essay competition is organised was greatly influenced by Indian literature, visible in his short stories like "The serpent and the candlestand of the bad offices." He even named his daughter Golconda after the famous fort of India.

The essays of this year's contest to be written in Spanish and English, is on Sinan as well Indo-Panamanian relations. One section of the contest is devoted to the translation of Sinan's poems and essay provided by the embassy into Hindi. The Spanish Language School of Jawaharlal Nehru University which ran into trouble for inviting LK Advani to release a Hindi-Spanish grammar book recently, has actively promoted the contest. The editor of the school's journal, Hispanic Horizons, Anil Dhingra has published a special number on the translations of Sinan which will be released on December 10.

Panama has been sending such indulgent ambassadors to India. Polo's predecessor Louis AguilarPonce was a painter of great repute who even picked up subjects from Indian streets during his stay in India and even represented his country in the last triennial.

Panama is little known in this country. Even the white packet of cigarettes by this name is out of fashion these day. But there is a lot of goodwill on both sides, courtesy some zealous enthusiasts like the present ambassador who has served her country in the early 80s as a junior diplomat in India, when India had not even set up a full Latin American division in the Ministry of External Affairs.

There may not be many Panamanians in India but Panama City is full of Indian's who own cinema halls, shops and hotels. This feature of Indian enterprise is prevalent in the whole of Central America. India needs to have a second look at its priorities about these region which continues to be on the backburner. There could not have been a more befitting tribute to Daulat Sinhji P Jadeja who can be tacitly termed as the original Indian Latin Americanist. He has been rightly chosen to be the chief guest at the December 10 function for his unrewarded services to the cause of Indo-Latin American relations.

Demolishing Language Barrier

The cocktail reception held by the ambassador of Argentina at her residence in Panchsheel Marg following a seminar on Argentinian writer Jorge Luis Borges was attended by diplomats, scholars, journalists and many students. The opening of the Indian economy might have diluted the Indian craze for *phoren* goods but the lure of *phoren* languages goes unabated. Almost every third student in Delhi picks up a diploma course in a foreign language—French, Italian, German or Spanish—in addition to normal degree pursuit. Many are making a serious career through these courses. At such a reception, I am normally introduced to students, who speak the language fluently, almost like a native.

The centre for Spanish studies at the school of languages in the Jawaharlal Nehru University has established itself as a vibrant link between India and the Hispanic world. Apart from churning out diploma and degree holders in Spanish language, it offers serious courses in Spanish and Latin American culture and society. The school produced a commemorative volume on one of the greatest Spanish writers Jorge Luis Borges who died in 1986 after almost a century of creativity expressed through poetry and prose both fictional and contemplative. The volume has been edited by Prof Anil Dhingra who can be aptly described as the rising Indian star on the Hispanic horizon.

In a short span of his editorship of the centre's journal by the same name, Dhingra has brought out special numbers on prominent writers from the Hispanic world such as Cesar, Valejo, Garcia Lorca and Rogelio Sinan. As a recognition to this untiring zeal and remarkable contribution in bridging the cultural gap between India and that part of the world, he will be decorated with a Panamanian honour in November this year.

The most interesting point of conversation I heard in the party was from journalist-cum-Hindi writer Vishnu Khare who surprised a group of Hispanic linguists that almost every Hindi writer from Manohar Shyam Joshi to BN Uniyal and from Shamsher Bahadur Singh to Kunwar Narain has bcen influenced by Borges which is apparent in their short stories and novels. The trend continues in the works of younger poets including Delay Prakash, Devi Prasad Mishra and Teji Grover. It belies the monopolistic puritanism of Indian Hispanic linguists as well as, I believe, other linguists too that writers of foreign languages can't be understood and appreciated in totality of nuances through translated works. If that were the case, how come every literary author of India has derived creative inspiration from Borges. I am sure many of them would have read works of Borges either in English or Hindi.

In fact, it is high time when language centres should take upon themselves to render great writers of the world into Indian languages and vice versa. The works of great writers would then be enjoyed by the masses too. That is the only way in which linguistic barriers can be demolished. Otherwise all linguistic literary endeavours will perhaps be confined to the seminar and committee rooms. It might bring laurels to the professors, but will not bring writers and literature closer to actual readers and genuine writers. Unlike Octavio Paz, Borges never came to India but he studied Indian philosophy and ethos which is reflected in many of his writings, informs Khare. He remained an agitated soul through out his creative life groping in the dark labyrinths of quintessential queries about life, existence and death. Said he once about himself, "I am scared to be. At times I feel I am unlucky and I start thinking; but how does all this matter. If it happened to one individual called Borges who lived in South America in the twentieth century, already so long ago? How does it matter if he was unlucky or unhappy if he has been forgotten already, if the century he lived has been forgotten, if his country has been forgotten, how does all this matter to me".

The other revelation on Borges was that his writing had traces of Jainism and Buddhism. According to ambassador Sampietro, soon a book will be published on Borges containing articles by Indian experts and scholars. It was heartening to note how foreign writers separated by continents and oceans are influenced by the philosophical contents of our seers and sages and in turn they inspire Indian writing today. Ever since this ambassador took charge, the annual essay competition has become quite popular among Indian students and other enthusiasts. Similarly, the modest newsletter called *News from Argentina* continues to inform and educate Indian readers in a most innovative way.

At the cocktail reception, I met the ever-ebullient Venezuelan ambassador Jocelyn Henrique King who has just returned from home after a long vacation. She was surprised like many of us Indians to find that Najma Heptullah lost the race to the vice-presidency and Salman Khurshid is still out of political reckoning.

But she seemed visibly impressed by the Indian ambassador to her country Niranjan Desai who despite initial apprehension about going to an alien land is doing a good job for his country. The evening had too many surprises in store for me like the former joint secretary Deb Brata Sana going to Indian Statistical Institute to take up a research project for his Ph.D. Academia does continue to attract people of all ages and denominations including the foreign service.

Lalit Mansingh and his Spice Girls

Ever since Lalit Mansingh has taken over as the secretary west in the ministry of External Affairs, there is an aura of cultural diplomacy and dignified informality in the air. This is especially true in the case of Latin American region which has been neglected for long by successive incumbents. But suddenly a great rapport is visible between South Block and the missions of this region in New Delhi. For this, credit should also be given to the new divisional head Homai Shah who with her unassuming style has already made a dent in our bilateral relations with 10-odd countries operating from New Delhi also.

It is a pleasant coincidence that the majority of Latin American ambassadors and their Indian counterpart happen to be women. One of them Elda B Sampietro was given a warm farewell by Lalit Mansingh in a hotel. I met both Lalit and Homai again on this occasion and guess who all came for the lunch, the numero uno beautiful fashion designer Ritu Beri who could give run for their money to her models on the ramp, Spanish linguist Vibha Maurya of Delhi University and hoardes of other Indian Latin Americanists. The only guest conspicuously absent was Sonal Mansingh. Courtesy the host, these farewells are no more a formal ritual as was the case earlier. There is an undercurrent of understanding and compassion between the diplomats on the two sides which seems to have been assiduously cultivated. I have been a witness to a couple of such efforts including the Christmas bash of the Venezuelan ambassador Figueora, the informal farewell to the former Chilean ambassador Hgueora, the Chilean national day and the likes. Argentina ranks among better related countries with India in the western hemisphere. Starting from Rabindranath in 1920s when he had to break his journey at Buenos Aires on his way to Peru and which culminated to a lifelong relationship with that country till the recent reciprocal visits of Carlos Menem and PV Narasimha Rao, we have covered a long distance. There are Argentine scholars such as Mariano Iturbe, Anasiri and Rudolf Berinejo interacting with Indians at Delhi and Jawaharlal Nehru Universities. There is the solitary joint venture between the two countries near Mathura which produces chemicals and finally an annual essay competition organised by the Argentina embassy which attracts a lot of Indians to reflect on the bilateral relations. On the other hand there is Anand Bhavan in Buenos Aires being run by Rene Marie Cura in the memory of late Victoria Ocampo who was the hostess and later an inspiration of Tagore whom he fondly called Bijoya. The miniscule Sikh farming community in northern Argentina which prompted Giani

Zail Singh's visit to that hamlet during his visit in the 1980s. There is an Indian chair in an Argentine university where our former ambassadors such as Moni Chaddha and Lakhan Mehrotra have had the honour to lecture on Indology.

At a more commercial level, the business between the two countries is growing at an encouraging pace with the help of individual entrepreneurs such as Casa Hindu in the Argentine capital. It is indeed high time that a reciprocal Argentine chair is established here in India. There is another area that binds the two countries spiritually but has remained unsung thanks to our secular dispensation. Planeloads of Argentine devotees of Sai Baba fly to Puttapurti in South India. It even includes their high profile ministers and parliamentarians. But we don't seem to be making any lasting capital out of this spiritual reservoir. If the travel agency in Argentina handling these pilgrimages could be cultivated to expand these trips towards the historical and cultural aspect of Indian tourism, we would be making a giant stride in promoting people to people relations.

What's French for Soccer?

Tennis, cricket and now football mania is ready to hit the world. France well known for its wine, cheese and excellent cuisine will host the 16th FIFA World Cup. Hosting a lunch that followed a press conference the French ambassador Claude Blanchemaison announced the French government's intention of making all relevant information available to the media as and when required during the World Cup.

If I have chosen to write about football this time in my column it is because the rage about this sport unlike cricket which is played by a handful of countries is such that it is a global phenomena. Thus, when globalisation is the most happening topic to be discussed at almost all the parties these days what better subject than football. Especially since the *babu moshais* in our country will be discussing the game for days to come.

But first a little bit more about the lunch. Needless to say the food was French and served in a way only the French can. Delicate bits of beans in excellent sauce, potatoes laced with seasoning were served complemented with wine. The variety of cheese that France produces is any country's envy.

Considering the amount of fans visiting the land of the country of Eiffel Tower, will be around 2.5 million spectators the French government is all set to entertain the fans to add thrill to the competition. From India the French embassy have already sponsored some lucky fans to be in France to watch the matches. There are 32 participating countries the favourite of course being Brazil followed by Italy. But other groups to watch for this time are South Korea which has a strong team and interestingly Nigeria according to a French official. Just for the record the 4.97 kilos of solid gold and malachite moulded into exquisite piece of object d'art was designed by Italian sculptor Silvio Gazzaniga.

All the parties that I have been attending discussions on the innumerable political parties in India, the change of government and from 10 Janpath will she won't she have been passe and diplomats from each countries are talking about football and the finer points of their football team back home.

The French embassy plans to install giant screens in stadiums and public places, so as to enable the fans to watch the game which will be telecast mostly during night. So it is goodbye to discos, parties and the social gatherings for now especially for the youth for whom the World Cup will be a special time to sit in front of these screens and scream hoarse for the winning team with chilled cold drinks and beer by the side whichever the lucky winning team may be. At the venue where the football matches will be played extreme precautions have been made to tackle violence among fans. Those who are lucky enough to be in France during the FIFA World Cup can look forward to not only safe football matches but a variety of other entertainments lined up for them that is if they get past their schedule of doing the usual round of tourist views as France is one of the leading countries in the world tourism does brisk business from the millions of people who visit is every year with or without the World Cup.

A Diplomat's Hospitality

The ambassadors rightfully expected to be great hosts because of the position and power they wield attending a party thrown by a middle order commercial diplomat and an educationist at their Vasant Vihar residence was a greater experience in hospitality and Indian indulgence. It was after a long time that I was invited by a diplomatic couple other than an ambassador in an informal setting of their lovingly assembled condominium. There was no familiar normal level in-that house. After entering from the road level, one had to take, a few steps down below while the hosts lived few steps above. The sitting space was intelligently divided into an informal "baithak" with mattresse and cushions and elongated side table for eateries and drinks and exclusive corner tete a tete in solitude with lots of ethnic Bedouin hangings. Food was delicious salad and pialla which is somewhat like the Indian non-vegetarian pulao with the exception being the dash of wine in it.

Mario Henrique Quinteros the then first secretary handling commercial affairs at the Argentine embassy and Ana Siri is an expert on Spanish language and literature, presenting interfacing with JNU and warm and sweet by nature. Prior to coming to India, Mario was posted in Kuwait, his interest and indulgence in the country of his posting was evident from the artistically choses mementos ranging from intricate maps to intensely knotted Bedouin carpets. Incidentally, Bedouin is a nomadic tribe found in Arabia and North Africa known for rearing horses and camels and its floating characteristics which is on decline now.

Latest trend shows that they are now opting for permanent settlements. Interestingly the tribe has a tradition of marrying within the clan which some biologists feel multiply the hereditary deficiency seen in many children of this tribe. It was very thoughtful of the hosts to offer a typical oriental setting to make them comfortable as against their rich Latin background. But the prize of the evening was the legendary Isabel El Kadi, who is genuinely identified with the Spanish presence in Delhi. The Hispanic enthusiasts in the Capital will vouch for her abiding interest in India and Indians with an unbelievable knowledge about the *catras* and *kuchas* of Chandni Chowk. She even offered very graciously to take me around the Old Delhi *gallies*. Though married to an Iraqi, she has adopted Delhi as her first home. Despite her ripe age, she drives all by herself in the late hours of evenings depicting her fate in the law and order situation of the Capital. One of her evincing interest is in all laughing matters which are predominantly Indian. Coming from the continent which is quasi tragic and quasi comic her amazement about the Indian capacity to laugh at itself is enormous.

The evening proved beyond doubt that India continues to attract foreigners of all hues and shapes because of its mullifaceted cultural kaleidoscope. And it is not a new phenomena. This very week the Argentine embassy in India brought out an eight page commemorative pull out on Victoria Ocampo who met Rabindranath Tagore in 1924 by providential accident when Tagore fell sick on his way to Peru and halted at Buenos Aires. Victoria played host to him and is known as *bijoya.*

It was the Argentine-way of participating in India's 50th year of Independence. Earlier this year in June, they had sent the pride of their navy ARA Libertade in the series of similar gestures. Brazil also displayed a similar sentiment when it also sent a similar ship to the Bombay coast. Sending ships in peacetimes to friendly countries is an age old custom to express solidarity and goodwill between the two concerned nations, especially so by the renowned naval powers, however Venezuela chose to release 12 postage stamps with Gandhi pictures.

These days, I am reading the book "In Light of India" by Noble Laureate Octavio Paz, who understood India during his stint as Mexican ambassador and who has now chosen to men down his perception on Ram and Allah, Apsara and Yakshi and Gandhi and Nehru. A must read for all those who are interested in India.

Saying Shalom to India

The Israel embassy provided Delhities with a thrilling glimpse of that country's culture last week while saying *shalom* to the 50th anniversary of Indian Independence. The cultural activities included a dance performance by the Hora dance troupe, a food festival, a fashion show and Israeli films.

The World Wide Friendship Association gave a reception for the Hora dance troupe which has about 20 young dancers (mostly in the age group of 16 to 28) at the Indian handicrafts emporium in Mehrauli, next to the Qutb Minar. This also marked the five years of established diplomatic relations between India and Israel. During this period, Israel has covered so much distance in various fields, which even most of the other countries operating here since Indian independence have been not able to do. This shows the tenacity of their purpose and will to come closer to this country, courtesy the historical links what with the Jewish community's presence here.

Israel, which came into being as a sovereign nation in 1946, has focused attention on the Jewish diaspora which was forced to spread to the four corners of the world because of sustained persecution at the hands of the other 'believers' as well as racial discriminators. But the Jews never faced any problems in India.

It's a different story that Jews on their own continued to migrate to US and even Israel during the period when India for the sake of its biggest minority had put all its eggs in the Arab basket. But all this is in the past. History has come full circle and even the Arabs are now willing to play ball with Israelis—the Palestine imbroglio notwithstanding. The last five years of formal Indo-Israeli diplomatic relations should be evaluated in this backdrop.

For the purpose of comparison it will be an interesting exercise to weigh this diplomatic growth with another new player - South Africa. Let's take a brief look. Both started direct flights, both also started publishing newsletters and other literature in a big way. If South Africans made their presence through their cricket team and the legacy of Mahatma Gandhi, Israeli's opened a cultural centre with heavily stuffed menu of films, teaching of Hebrew language and an exposure to Judaism.

'Shalom India' kaleidoscope was the culmination of the efforts of the jovial and articulate Israeli ambassador Yehoyada Haim and his talented team. Narrating the homework which went into the organisation of the Hora dance troupe and other activities like the food festival, the intellectual dialogue, fashion show, photo exhibition etc. ambassador Haim told a packed Siri Fort auditorium before lighting the traditional lamps with Indian Council for Cultural Relations director general Himachal Som.

I developed cold feet when a suggestion was made that I should bring out folk dancers for Indian audience. It was like selling "Ice to Alaska." The next two hours proved how modest the ambassador was trying to be. The folk dance numbers drawn from everyday life of Israel kept the thousand-strong spectators spellbound. The new DC, Som, deserves full credit for facilitating such an eventful Israeli presentation. Ever since he was called from his ambassadorial posting in Laos to takeover as the head of ICCR—the calender of events have multiplied, both in content and quality.

Coming back to the World Wide Friendship reception, both the host and the venue were pleasant surprises for me. To the delight of the Israeli dancers, Kathak duo sisters Kamalini and Nalini gave a performance under the veteran guru Jitender Maharaj. This brought the Israeli cameras out of the bags. A young and pretty dancer by the name of Nama with whom I was talking begged leave to be in the front to see the footwork of the dancers.

The guests were also entertained with impromptu dance by the Hora dance troupe. Some of them promptly learnt the dance and joined them, igniting a real friendship. There are many friendship associations functioning in Delhi but this one under the leadership of Som seems to be the most active one. It was certainly taking the necessary pains to make both the guests from home and abroad comfortable. One must have passed by the Indian handicrafts emporium dozens of times, but the inside ambience, ideally suited for an evening reception as well as multi-dimensional permanent exhibits of ethnic handicrafts and sculptures, was an unprecedented delight for which the chairman of the reception committee Om Prakash must be given all kudos.

Of Parties and Delegates

By now it is abundantly clear to me that South Block has vertically divided the globe. One set of nations is those with which it wants to maintain warmer than normal relations and the second is of the run-of-the-mill category. The two sets are manifested by the level of Indian participation in their national day celebration. For the first category, it sends the Vice-President and the Lt Governor of Delhi for the second. The Central Asian Republics continue to be in the exalted company of the former as was the case some time ago at the national day of the Kazakhstan republic where Krishan Kant stayed put for almost the entire proceedings. Kazakh ambassador Rashid Ibraev has been in Delhi now for over two years. During this period, he and his wife Assyly Khan have earned the reputation of being one of the most elegant diplomatic couples in town. Even their daughter is conspicuous by her stunning presence in such parties. A lot of things have happened during the stint of ambassador Ibraev. Earlier, he surprised Indian President KR Narayanan by presenting him a carpet with his picture woven on it.

His president Noor Sultan A Nazarbaev paid an official visit in 1996. Soon after Ibraev took over as the ambassador, the then Vice-President KR Narayanan paid a visit to Kazakhstan. Ispat Karmet—one of the largest steel plants in former Soviet Union—has started functioning at an awe-inspiring capacity of 6 million tonnes per annum producing coke to tin plates and even graduating fast to generate its installed capacity of 435 megawatts. Ibraev constantly feeds the prospective Indian investors about the great potential his country holds for entrepreneurs. Incidentally, Kazakhstan with an area of 27 million sq km is larger than the entire Western Europe in size.

India is already collaborating in areas such as mining, electronics, infrastructure, medicine and agriculture. A joint bank and trade houses have been opened, weeks of business cooperations have been organised and with the plans of trans-Asian railway through Turkmenistan and Iran upto Mumbai holds great prospects for bilateral economic relations.

Coming back to the party, it was a pleasant surprise to see hundreds of Indian businessmen intermingling with the Central Asian diplomats which spoke volumes about Indian enterprise and the credibility they enjoy with the former Soviet brethren. One of the regulars at these parties is the former chief of army staff K Sundarji who is ageing gracefully – without losing his good old touch. It is but natural that Bofors returns to one's mind at the mere reference of the general and he is always ready with a repartee the moment you mention the subject. Says he that the last word is yet to come on the subject.

I must add here that I was a witness to a very interesting conversation between the beautiful Mrs Sundarji who looked radiant in a red saree that complimented her fair complexion. She wanted to know why some of the invitees had come dressed in casuals. She especially came down heavily on Indian journalists who did not respect the dress code suggested (lounge suit in this case) in the invitation card. That brings to the fore the issue of the dress code.

Interestingly, I have been observing that many journalists and even professors of illustrious universities including the Jawaharlal Nehru University do not follow the dress code, yet stand out in their smart casuals amidst three piece suits and simmering sarees. Checking this out with fellow journalists, I was told that generally they came straight from work as the evening receptions clash with deadlines. Perhaps it is also possible journalists in their initial days could not afford the luxury of lounge and dinner suits.

Alternatively, they are expected to wear the national dress. Now what is the Indian national dress? Let's begin with our first President Rajinder Prasad who wore a long coat with a modest dhoti and a white Gandhi cap. He was succeeded by philosopher President Radhakrishnan who opted for a Tamilian turban. Then came the educator-turned-statesman Zakir Hussain who wore a churidar and a sherwani. In fact all Indian Presidents have their own preferences ranging from *bandh galas* of VV Giri and Venkatraman minus the cap. Compared to this, our present Prime Minister does't bat an eyelid in sporting a suit and tie even while representing the nation abroad. This again pops up the question what is our national dress and how could it be possible with culture, climate, language, dress code and the eating habits changing after every 50 kilometres from Kashmir to Kanniyakumari. Yes there is a dress code in the former world of Sundarji's where the men and officers wear the same uniform on all frontiers and even at peace stations of the country. Therefore Mrs Sundarji's disgust about Indian journalists, I guess, is understandable.

Occassion-Free Interaction should be Encouraged

It was again a farmhouse tucked in the by-lanes of Vasant Kunj, the same World Wide Friendship Society of SS Soin fame and the same friendly diplomatic fraternity gathering on a Sunday afternoon to have the last glimpses of the fast receding sunny winter afternoon. But with a difference.

While driving through the maze of the Vasant Kunj backyard I had an eerie feeling, courtesy the screaming headlines about the recent onslaught on these farmhouses by some infamous criminal tribes operating in the Outer Delhi. The sociologists of the intellectual world would I like to convince me about the social injustice and inequitable distribution of wealth in India, manifest through the opulent and at times vulgar farmhouses. But, is the endless wailing on our penury the answer? I am amazed at the opposition to the biggest ever cake on display this Sunday to mark the 50th year of our Independence under the pretext that same food could have fed thousands of impoverished and hungry people—as if, had this cake not been made, the material used would have all reached empty bellies. Anyway, going back to the fellowship lunch hosted by the WWFS for no particular rhyme or reason was yet another example of the untiring zeal and enthusiasm on the part of Soin and his friends to bring foreign diplomats posted in New Delhi closer to Delhi-ites at large. Mixing freely with the diplomats were Indian ladies and children, who enjoyed the variety of cultural programmes provided for their entertainment.

I feel this is the best way to avoid the recent unfortunate incident, involving an Indian journalist and an African diplomat's wife. Such innocuous and occasion-free interaction can really help in shedding off the in-built inhibitions towards a coloured or a white skinned person, which is deeply ingrained in the mind of an ordinary Indian. The organisers had gone out of their way in serving a sumptous buffet lunch, preceded by a stream of liquid diets capped by *jalebi* and *rabri*. The sprawling lawns of Savannah Gardens, the venue, is one of the many readymade backward spaces which have sprung up in all parts of the country, fulfilling a long-felt gap for formal and informal get togethers.

The Delhi-based diplomatic community is generally intrigued at the fast changing political scenario at Raisina Hills where a saffron-led government is all set to takeover.

The most disturbed are the Pakistani and the Chinese diplomats, at the prospective political dispensations but for different reasons. An ordinary Pakistani considers the Hindu nationalist BJP to have a hawkish streak in an otherwise soothing secular rainbow. But the same Atal Behari Vajpayee has at least proved that his world-view is in tandem with the consensus foreign policy, laid down by Jawaharlal Nehru.

But the Chinese have a lot to worry about. The border dispute has been swept under the carpet for the time being but not the Dalai Lama factor which has spiritual overtones, apart from those relating to national self-respect. My Chinese friends in Delhi force me to believe that the disappearance of the Dalai Lama factor would pave the way for a better bilateral relationship.

I am sorry to point out that the same thing was said some nine years ago when Rajiv Gandhi took the bold initiative of putting the Sino-Indo border dispute on the backburner. We continue to compete, rather than supplement, in world trade. Even the much touted trade fair last year could not open more bargaining counters for Indian and Chinese goods for each other.

But our relationship is on an even keel despite Dalai Lama and his Tibetan followers, spread over the length and breadth of this country. When I asked a cultural counsellor officer, while having an informal lunch, that will they give us our land in lieu of Dalai Lama, he promptly shot back—will we put Arunachal on the plate along with Dalai Lama.

Partying the Night Away

When I was invited to this innocuous sounding party called *Next Wave* at the Okhla industrial complex I did not think much about the prospects. But since a close friend insisted I decided to spend a late evening. It turned out to be like a film of the famous Italian director Federico Felini who is known for juxtaposing scenes from life and weaving them in his own grammar which bore this exclusive stamp.

The guests included a very conscious Udham Singh VJ of Channel V sporting his famous earring but minus *Kambal* and *the lathi,* who has given currency and credence to the land of the Lals in Indian politics—Haryana. For the first time in seven years of my marriage I too feel proud of the ancestry of my in laws. From Indian politics to the terrace of PJ Singh of Headstart fame these Haryanavis have come a long way. Lo and behold he was accompanied by a friendly neighbourhood, literally and figuratively – Manpreet Brar. My friend who spoke to her was in high praise and really found her down to earth despite her celebrity status. Then there was a sprinkling of have been stars like Abhinav *Nanhe* Chaturvedi of *Hum Log,* but what caught my immediate fancy was the sprinkling of foreign diplomats of all colours and of all generations.

The party actually began at the stroke of midnight when the guests, who were all over the place, on the three floors what I believe is supposed to be the business spaces of the ad agency Headstart and the marketing consultants and researchers—Admark. Some people were dancing both close and formal, some were tucked away in discreet and not so discreet corners and some I heard got busy seeing films later leaving many dazed as to what kind of a film that would be.

Despite a regular and generous flow of liquor and a sumptuous buffet spread, no one was in a tearing hurry to eat or to go home. I have never seen such a large variety of guests feeling at home in an Indian parly which had a variety on show from dance to music, wives to accompanied partners and *kurta pyjamas* to three piece suits. It was a day when the destiny of a country was being rewritten at Raisina Hill by the first citizens of India but no one could care less whether Atal Bihari had received the invitation to form the government except a dignified old lady who later turned out to be the mother of Boney Duggal of whose birthday the party was organised. She said with a transparent honesty that she had been praying for Vajpayee to be the next Prime Minister in her opinion in the entire part he was the only best bet.

That was the only serious comment I picked the whole evening. But my best evening was spent watching Shamiak Davar and his troupe who performed at the hotel Le Meridien as part of the hotel's tenth anniversary. After the dinner a sumptuous dinner was served. The party included a number of ambassadors and diplomats,

A lot has been written about the size of the cake and decorations, but the main attraction I must say was the scintillating performance of Davar and his group who danced and sung numbers in all possible languages. At last we have a desi troupe which sends even firangs gyrating.

B'bye India, Hello China

When the 34 Latin American nations were trying to create a free trade area in the Western hemisphere in the Chilean capital Santiago back home, in New Delhi a Latin American ambassador Joclyn Henrique de King of Venezuela was packing up to leave for Beijing after an eventful stint in India. It was almost the same time when the President of India KR Narayanan was also preparing to embark on an I unprecedented 15-day-tour of two Latin American countries—Peru and Brazil.

Much water has flown down the Yamuna river since the time Jocelyn arrived in India about four years ago. It was manifest in the friends she made during this period who came to bid her goodbye at a sombre farewell reception on the spacious lawns of her residence at 24, Prithviraj Road.

The news of the demise of Mexico's most famous poet Octavio Paz made the reception even more sombre, though this time Jocelyn's guest included a new friend—the actor-turned-member-of-Parliament, Vinod Khanna who stood chatting with a group of men in one corner, most probably discussing Jayalalitha's antics.

A beautiful decorated elephant, which had almost became a regular feature in her parties stood flapping its large ears as an Indian *barat* band belted out popular Hindi numbers while she tried to be as mirthful as possible barely hiding the melancholy on her face on leaving the country with which she forged an instant rapport. Her assortment of friends included beauty contestants, charity collectors, Parliamentaries, erstwhile royalties, socialites, tennis coaches and of course diplomats and journalists.

She should not be unfamilier to the readers of this column as she has figured where umpteen number of times. But this was a different occasion. It was one time she was not only a generous hostess but also the centre of attraction herself as she knew that this was perhaps her last meeting with so many friends at the same time.

Jocelyn will be remembered by friends and acquaintances in India as an undiplomatically-straight person who minced no words in calling a spade. At one level she loved India for its ancient civilisation, its vast geographical expanse and the variety of the people but at the same time she did not like the patronising attitude of some officials and many other self-styled experts.

She knew her limitations despite her best efforts and intentions, the bilateral relations could not take a dramatic turn. But I am definitely certain that at a people-to-people contact level, she was more than successful in bringing the two countries together. She will be remembered for a long time to come by all those who were lucky to have known her intimately. For reasons beyond mundane diplomacy and officiallese.

Of Thai Cuisine

Some time ago I had mentioned about the importance of food in diplomacy with particular reference to the popularity of Chinese cuisine in India. Of late many other countries of South Asia are also taking a cue from their big neighbour. It is the turn of Thai Food now. A new Thai food restaurant, the *Sprice Root* was recently inaugurated, (the decor must be seen to be believed). The Best Western Surya is also holding a Thai food festival. I must mention, the food there was really nice, re-invoking nostalgia for a taste that only my grandmother was able to dish out. I had long forgotten the taste. The soup though I found was the best part.

The name are too exotic to list here but many of the dishes—especially one dish I had was of cauliflower and potato—reminded me of Indian curry that went especially well with dry chill power chutney. Sounds familier ? It should be for the Thais just like Mexicans and Indians are avid users of spices.

Live Carol Band and Smiling, Santa for CRY Kids

It is celebration lime. There are parties everywhere and the spirit of the festival is overwhelming. As usual, the ambassador of Venezuela, Jocelyn Henrique de King, gave a Christmas eve party that was well attended by diplomats, friends and socialites. The traditional Christmas fare she serves with excellent choice of cheese and wine was relished by all. But the best party attended then was at the lawns of Ashoka, ITDC, organised by the staff and hosted by Vice-President M Manchanda. It was a special party for the children of CRY and Missionaries of Charity, one I am sure the children will remember for years to come. The Christmas party included a live carol hand, a puppet show, a magic show, some games, a four tiered cake with a smiling Santa, to be devoured by the kids of course, and lots of goodies.

The Panamanian ambassador, Mina S Polo, herself a philanthropist graced the happy occasion as she watched children prancing around the lawn with mouths full and balloons in their hands. Later, they lined up to sing 'jingle bells' and receive gifts from Santa, was told that ITDC has been organising the Christmas party every year since 1994. Seeing the joy on the faces of these children was indeed an overwhelming experience.

There is a subtle diplomacy this hotel practices. Ashok was built when there were not many five star hotels around to share the diplomatic pie in the Capital. Despite the stiff competition, it continues to don the mantle on the official host for the endless heads of state and their delegations every month. It has, in fact, earmarked the Naga, the Nataraja, Neelam and the Panna suits on its fifth floor exclusively for the foreign dignitaries. Its sprawling convention hall and the lush green compound around the swimming pool have hosked numerous conferences. Many foreign delegates invited by the Indian government, it was one of the first to open a Japanese restaurant Tokyo, the one and only, which serves authentic Japanese food, displays waxed look alike replicas of the food outside the entrance of the restairant as is done everywhere in Japan and provides tatami mats lor seating. "We do send our chef to Tokyo every once in a while to be in touch with traditional Japanese food," says Manjula Arun, the public relations manager. While the hotel may boast of being the only authentic one in Japanese cuisine, which of course most Japanese may agree to, there is just one thing that the restaurant may have to look into and that is the transportation of the sea food which is the hallmark of any Japanese dish. "I'll feel more comfortable if the same could arrive a wee bit early from whichever coastal town they are "brought" says the chief of Bank of Tokyo in India, who visits the restaurant often and whom I happened to meet at the reception held on the occasion of the birthday of Bhutanese king Jigme Singe Wangchuk at the Bhutanese embassy. A sentiment echoed by the Japanese ambassador too! Understandable, there is no sea in Delhi.

The Japanese are here in a big way with their Hondas, Suzukis. Sonys and Casios. But the ambassador is not happy. He feels that is not enough though they have made the fourth largest investment in this country. Still they rightfully envy the presence of the neighbouring Koreans in the Indian corporate sector. The forthcoming visit of the Japanese foreign minister in the second week of the New Year, the first after ten years will sort out many knotty issues between the two countries. India has recently suffered a humiliating defeat at the hands of the Japanese at the security council's non-permanent members elections. India is putting up a brave face as if nothing has happened but this has to be shown by some concrete actions to salvage the hurt, the Indian popular opinion has suffered.

The large presence of the Indian business and academic community at the Japanese emperor's birthday celebrations recently was a pointer that nothing much is wrong between us. On this occasion, the government of Japan announced the conferment of "the order of the rising sun gold rays with Rossette" to Professor Satya Bhusan Sharma of Jawaharlal Nehru University in recognition to the meritorious service by teaching Japanese language since 1947.

Learning Cultural Diplomacy, the Hard Way

Yanni, the Greece-born-American-composer, and it little earlier the immortal British playwright Shakespeare taught a lesson or two to the modern practitioners of international diplomacy. Ever since the hard bargaining in bilateral trading has given a mild tush to the traditional diplomacy, culture had taken a backseat. Gone are the days of the festivals of India which had travelled to China, France and even America. Few year ago when we are celebrating the 50 year of independence, one is surprised at the total absence of any such initiative. Shocking as it may be, but nevertheless true, that British and the Americans are coming here to participate in our celebrations. But do we have anything to show to the world. It was a gracious gesture of the reigning queen Elizabeth of Britain to lend, us the fabulous painting of the Shah Jahan period of *Padshanmah.*

Though it could be described as a tribute of one royalty to the other. It did attract hoards of Indians making a beeline to the national museum where they were exhibited.

The same Shah Jahan was further glorified when the world renowned musician Yanni chose Taj Mahal as the backdrop for spreading the message of love. The glitterati of Delhi and Mumbai was present in its best to give out standing ovation to an artist who sold India to Indians. It reminded us of Peter Brook who retold *Mahabharata* in France and Richard Attenborough who reincarnated Gandhi on celluloid. All these examples must be included in any proposed book on Indian diplomacy.

The roads to Agra couldn't have been more busier with Mercedes, Hondas, Cielos and Fords zooming to and fro at high speeds. The hotels were all booked to capacity and those who could listen to Yanni's music could not stop raving about being transposed to another ethereal world.

India is not alone in fidgeting when it comes to break new grounds for projecting its image which is one of the prime functions of modern day diplomacy. Is publishing glossy newsletters and holding cocktail parties sufficient? In fact, the number of such countries opting for alternative strategies in image building is fast increasing. These parties have become as reach as the word cocktail itself, where guests of varying indifference come to be spotted not by diplomats but by the fellow guests, reminiscent of similar gatherings at any cultural evening. These guests manage to include themselves in all mailing lists.

Not much can be said about the Indian cinema too, which has failed in the international arena, though we can talk about *Salam Bombay* and *Bandit Queen,* but they project a particular class of society, and is helping to promote cultural diplomacy in any way. With exceptions to few names such us Satyajit Ray, Shekhar Kapoor and Raj Kapoor, very few have been able to take Indian cinema to the heart of the international audience. It's time the rules of cultural diplomacy are re-written, Shakespeares and Yannis are telling us how to do it. Before Baba Sehgals and Apache Indians are declared as our official cultural envoys, we need to pull up our socks otherwise more than half of the Indian embassies would be rendered defunct. Trade and economy are to underline the contours of our diplomacy, then perhaps not more than dozen missions are required.

Some of the smaller countries like Israel, Italy and Greece have done a remarkable job in recent past. They were ably supported by the islands of academic activities undertaken by overzealous individuals.

Unfortunately, the reciprocal Indophiles are becoming a hopeless minority. Indian Council of Cultural Relations should concentrate on them. We can make a beginning from Africa from where more than 10,000 students are present in Indian universities at any given point of time after getting heavily subsidised tertiary degrees. They go back home to high positions in their own countries, and that should be our catchment we have invested in them.

The Bamboo Curtain Rises

There was a time when the sprawling Chinese diplomatic complex, uncomfortably adjacent to its American counterpart, used to invite indifference and apathy as an aftermath of the 1962 war. Even a genuine visit to the embassy could become a nightmare in the form of incessant police enquiries. The times have changed.

There is a perceptible change in the style and content of the Chinese diplomats posted in New Delhi. The diplomats, including the ambassador, used to wear light grey uniform even in formal receptions. What the embassy dished out for journalists and China watchers was nothing but insipid pamphleteering.

At a reception thrown to welcome the new Chinese cultural counsellor Jiang Wei Ming, everything looked different. Another newly arrived media chief Zao Xingmin spoke English like a British, courtesy his last posting in London. His wife, a dainty lady who spoke little English, aggressively tried to find out about the Indian society. "How many children do Indian couples have in India?" she asked, then rather informatively said, "in China, we have one child except in the countryside." When I replied it was almost the same in India except that couples here opted for two children, she asked, "why are the boys in India treated better than girls?" Phew! She wanted to know more and more, expressing her desire in remarkably well modulated gestures and bit of English.

At the party, the guest list as well as the Chinese menu was as elaborate as the present day Chinese foreign policy with all dimensions included. The dull pamphlet had been replaced by the glossy *Beijing Review* copies which covered all subjects under the sky. Liquor flowed endlessly.

Even the Buddhist Tibet was presented as a modern political entity, oblivious of Dalai Lama's influence in the rest of the world.

The same Chinese cultural centre had shown a series of documentary films, made by the noted commentator and film-maker Sawant showing the modern development in Tibet. Now it has been replaced by Hong Kong, Taiwan and Macau.

Chinese diplomats in India have a tricky brief. They know that India has agreed to put the border disputes on the backburner but have not forgotten it completely. It keeps on visiting them like a bad dream. Recently, Arunachal Pradesh chief minister Apang was denied a visa to China to participate in an international conference on biodiversity. The argument given was that Arunachal was a disputed territory between India and China. Hence Beijing could not afford to legitimise the Indian occupation of the state by granting a visa and that too to an elected chief minister. From the Chinese point of view, the argument was quite valid but it also proves that the back-burner theory was only for India. As far as China was concerned, it was willing to forget the dispute till India doesn't claim its land.

Chinese diplomats here prefer to remain silent on the matter. It is not their brief to enter into its argument on the issue. That is broader issue to be settled between the two governments at the highest level.

Their assignment is to improve the bilateral relations without taking into account any outstanding issue. They know the people on both sides have remained incommunicado for long because of historical reasons.

When history becomes road block, the saner course is to ignore it. A career diplomat's stint is too short to correct historical aberrations. He has to carry the baton during the space of his leg only, just like a participant in a quadrangular relay race.

That brings back the question of career diplomats versus those drawn from the public life. While the former could afford to spend his tenure in a status quoist manner, but the latter has to perform in order to make his mark.

Since he is in a hopeless minority, he ends up having a confrontation with the majority of the foreign service. This rarely happens in case of large countries such as China who only sends career diplomats at positions other than the ambassador.

Coming back to the party, it was heartening to note that all Chinese farewell at the buffet table, though Chinese no more fight shy in serving their American coke.

Incidentally, Libyan president Colonel Gadaffi. Once flashed a bottle of coke in an all-Arab conference as the symbol of neo-colonialism.

If you ask them why they will sheepishly tell you because you Indians love it so much. But their authentic Chinese food didn't get with our plates because our Indo-Chinese food sold and served at every nook and corner of the city has numbed out taste buds!

Mexican Charmer

The Brazilian national day celebration sadly had to be held inside the ambassador's residence because of the unpredictable Delhi monsoon. Monsoon for some particular reason had chosen the same day for an unabashed downpour. It was followed by the grand bash again of the Mexican national day celebration at Hyatt.

Guests comprising of diplomats, dignitories, businessmen academicians and a fair mix of media mingled around sipping champagne, scotch and tequila, the all too familiar Mexican drink that can hit you straight if you are not used to it. And all this while, a live band sporting sombrero belted out songs that couldn't keep the guests still. Of course, the songs included Tequila and Lambada.

Arriving just a year ago, the Mexican ambassador, Edmundo Font, has had the ladies go ga ga over his looks. "One could easily fall in love with him" cooed a lady journalist while he shook hands with his counterparts at the party. But it is not just his looks that need mentioning in this column. He recently released a book of poems that has been the topic of conversation for months now.

Unfortunately, I have not had the opportunity to read the book as I have been unable to get hold of it. But since I have a fascination for Latin American writers, having read over and over again Colombian writer Marquez's Hundred years of Solitude, Pablo Neruda's poems and other contemporary short stories, my impatience is really heating up.

While talking about Latin American writers, I must mention the ex-Colombian ambassador, David Sanchez Juliao who wrote beautiful short stories. A small library in the Colombian embassy contains all his stories.

Mexico party also reminded one of former Mexican ambassador to India, Pedro the insisted that he be addressed by his name, who could talk for hours on Hinduism without getting tired. The most missed ambassador in this party was ambassador of Somalia who seemed to be out of station for some reason.

Then came the Chilean party, again a celebration of the national day, a rather private and a formal affair followed again by Belize's national day. The Belize's consul, Mohinder Salmi never ceases to amaze me. His efforts have actually made Indians aware of Belize which, until recently, was known to only a few. And if you think it is only the Indians who didn't know about this small South American country then you are wrong. For just recently a Central Asian diplomat remarked he knew of Belize only after he knew of its Consul in India. "My sporadic interaction with Sahni has made me realise that he is a hardcore businessman by profession but his humility coupled somewhat with an informal element can easily melt anybody's heart and ditto for his wife too!"

South African High Commission announced a blitzkrieg named 'hitting sixes and fours', on the Indian media. Of course you guessed it right, the theme is cricket. It was launched on the eve of Gandhi's birthday. They couldn't have chosen a better day as Gandhiji had begun his historical journey of non-violence which finally saw the ousting of the British from India, from South Africa. Indeed it was a high tribute.

On right now at the Chanakya theatre is the film by Shyam Benegal, *The making of the Mahatma*—a film on the years of Mahatma in South Africa.

The President of the National assembly of the people's power, Cuba, visited India. New envoys of France, Uganda and Khyrgistan presented their credentials.

On the cultural scene, Mexico invited friends and connoisseurs to an exhibition of paintings by Eduardo Nunez Valbuena. The exhibition was inaugurated by Satish Gujral, famous Indian painter who spent some time in Mexico and returned with a strong Mexican influence, depicted on his murals. The embassy, along with the Indian Council for Cultural Relations also organised Mexican choreographer dancer Regina Quintero's 'Arala—island of her Heart' which was performed at Kamani.

Wang (Cultural Section) of Chinese embassy introduced Brig Sawant, the producer of two travelogues on Tibet which was screened for a select gathering at the embassy.

Australia is celebrating its millennium with several cultural activities.

The Guests Who didn't Come to Dinner

It may sound incredible but there is a large section of society who as a matter of convention or compulsion does not attend diplomatic parties despite being invited. In my five-year-odd exposure to these celebrations. I have never noticed an Indian uniformed officer. Though there are many ambassadors and diplomats who done their freshly ironed dresses and brass decorations and epauleets. Indian olive greens never show up—not even in farewells of military attaches. Same goes for IB and RAW officers. I have not even spoiled a police or a paramilitary officer in diplomatic receptions.

It is not that they are not invited. Every other day we hear of a Joginder Singh or a TR Kakkar attending an Interpol seminar in Lyonns or London.

That is acceptable in the professional confines but wining and dining with 'diplomats is a different matter. Ever since a RAW officer was sent back to India for hobnobbing with the Americans. Indian diplomats have become careful while accepting these invitations. Except for the concerned territorial division, the other officers excuse themselves politely.

Every embassy invites from President down to under-secretaries, with whom they interact. While the first citizen never obliged, the one in the making—Vice-President KR Narayanan—accepted most, readily. Narayanan was the chief guest at most places, second only to the incumbent Lt Governor and chief minister of Delhi, dressed usually in impeccable starched white dhoti and flashing raw silk kurta.

Generally, Vice-President's office forwards all invitations to the South Block for advise, but Narayanan accepted many requests on his won. Many a times it became embarrassing for the Lt Governor's office as no decision was taken even till the last minute.

Also, I have never been able to spot any Cabinet minister at these parties. Though Ministers of stale like RL Bhatia did oblige when they were in office. Once when Bhatia arrived to attend Pakistani national day celebrations, there was no chair earmarked for him. This was so because, firstly, they were not expecting him and also because they decided impromptu to do away with the tradition of offering the guest of honour status. How convenient!

It had created a furore in the Parliament. Though Bhatia put up a brave front saying he didn't feel insulted or humiliated, the then secretary (West) Vinod Grover called the then Pakistan high commissioner Riaz Khokar in his office to convey the displeasure.

Notable exception to this general rule is the present human resource development minister SR Bommai who not only attends almost all diplomatic parties but all what is offered. Even foreign secretaries rarely attend such functions. I can remember only JN Dixit and that too in the Bhutanese reception. Bhutan is marked as a sensitive one for obvious reasons.

Of late, top functionaries of the Bharatiya Janata Party (BJP) have also started showing up at these parties. Soon after relinquishing his office as Prime Minister, Atal Behari Vajpayee was seen at the Mauritian national day party—might be to express solidarity with the Indian dominated island nation in the Indian Ocean. But so did the Lok Sabha Speaker PA Sangma. Though such occasions are rare but one should not be surprised if next time one stumbles upon KR Malkani, as I did recently.

There are some who are regular fixtures at such parties. These can often be seen at Indian International

Centre or for concerts at the Indian Council for Cultural Relations and even a National School of Drama watching a play.

How these people wangle their way through is a mailer of great research. Nihal Singh has written a novel on the suhject and once Amita Malik spilled the beans in one of her columns. But, generally, they are ignored. What is most surprising is that these coveted hosts-never take the trouble of inviting Indian scientists, scholars, noted authors and top editors.

Even a beat correspondent from the ministry of external affairs rarely finds time to attend to them. The reason being the timing of these parties clash with the filing of stories and it is quite monotonous to rub same shoulders time and again.

One ambassador recently told me that they prefer inviting the real stuff exclusively, either at their homes or in five star hotels because no meaningful dialogue can take place in a crowd of hundred.

The guest feels ignored and the whole purpose is lost. Perhaps, that is why many Western nations choose to divide their invitees into various groups of like minded people or with similar professional interest. Also, at the end of the day both the host and guests should feel that the whole exercise was worth it.

But there is one category of guest which has no choice but to attend all receptions even if there are half a dozen in one evening. They are fellow ambassadors. If an ambassador doesn't accept invitation of his counterpart, it would be taken as a diplomatic amiss.

Not many like to dress up every evening to smile endlessly though that is considered to be a vital part of their protocol and function.

Desert Flavours in the Capital

Diplomatic parties in Delhi are not known for the political level of its guests barring the notional presence of the Vice-President or the Lt Governor of Delhi. But this week I attended a joint celebration of the 50th anniversary of India's independence by the Arab embassies in the capital. Guess who came for dinner that night? The most important woman of the Indian establishment, Sonia Gandhi. It is evident that she is trying very hard to play the roles destiny has bestowed upon her as the president of the oldest political party of India, the Indian National Congress. Diplomatic crowd is not unfamiliar to Sonia who is her capacity as the chairperson of Rajiv Gandhi Memorial Trust, she has been dealing with the high and mighty of the world politics and diplomacy.

But so far she has been the hostess to the likes of Julius Nyerara and Jomo Kenyata while in the Arab party, she was the focal point.

Arabs have maintained cordial relations with India despite the recent developments in the bilateral arena with Israel, barring a few exceptions like Syria and Lebanon. Arabs by and large are reconciled to the changing ground reality in West Asia. The evening party organised at Kamal Mahal in Maurya Sheraton was the epitome of Arab hospitality for a large gathering of Indians from all possible sections of society including the media. The invitations were sent out in the name of the ambassador of the United Arab Emirates who happens to be the dean of the Arab diplomatic community in New Delhi. The master of the ceremonies was the Palestinian ambassador whom I had spotted at the lobby of Maurya discussing the details with the staff of the hotel. The other important event of the week was the Israel's celebrations of their golden jubilee of their independence where also another rising star of the Indian establishment namely the new state minister for external affairs Vasundhara Raje made an unprecedented appearance.

Very rarely do Indian foreign ministers, grace such occasions but coming from the BJP household, Vasundhara made a loud and clear statement in favour of Indo-Israeli relations which are on an upward swing ever since the two countries have entered into full fledged relationship a couple of years ago.

The other guests at Le Meridien included the latest actor turned politican Vinod Khanna and the enfante terrible of Indian politics Subramaniam Swamy.

We were told at the party Israeli trade with India has crossed the $700 m mark. Only behind the US. They have already set up joint ventures.

The food served was exquisite and flown in all the way from Israel. The party and all the fun and frills by way of music and dance gave the country's distinctive flavour.

But interestingly many Israeli women wore sarees and mingled with the Indian women. If we go by the media presence one can easily say that the ambassador of Israel along with the most efficient press chief Gill Haskel are the most popular diplomat hosts in town.

Not All that Black

The Cuban embassy hosted a diplomatic party which was capable of washing away the image of all stereotype parties. It was organised on the second floor terrace of the India International Centre to mark the triple occasion of the Indo-Cuban friendship society, a painting exhibition by post-revolution painters of Cuba and a film show on the pre-revolution times.

There were no diplomats in it, no socialites or even social climbers. The guests included the common people who had gathered to express solidarity with Cuba.

India and Cuba have been natural allies through the period of Cold War. We don't need a friendship society, in fact, because both Indian and Cuban societies have co-existed sharing common goals and aspirations expressed through Non-Alignment and anti-imperialism despite long distances of language and geography. Frankly speaking, Cuba is the only Latin American country which has a political relationship with India. Cuba has a captive constituency in India in both the major communist parties who are sharing power at the centre in New Delhi.

Senior communist leaders including Jyoti Basu, Harkishen Singh Surjeet, Inderjit Gupta and AK Bardhan have shared platforms with the successive Cuban ambassadors and even Fidel Castro. That way, the present ambassador Olga Chamero Trias is lucky to be representing her country when the power elite in New Delhi is more than sympathetically inclined towards Havana in its crusade against the American blockade. It is the same leadership which had dispatched the shiploads of foodgrains in the hour of crisis during Rao regime.

Olga has made full use of her political friends in the Indian establishment today. India has already released commemorative stamp on Jose Marti, named a school after him on the Ring Road in RK Puram and is all set to observe the 30th martyrdom anniversary of Che Guevara which is next on the agenda of the Cuban embassy here. Recently, a professor of journalism at the Indian Institution of Mass Communication KM Srivastava returned with an entirely different picture from a 4-day stay in Havana in Cuba. According to him, the skyline of the Cuban capital is not at all that jet-black as it is being painted by the American press. The department stores are full with goodies and customers, the law and order situation is better than any other Latin American country today. American tourists continue to throng the Cuban streets and Cuban cigars continue to be consumed by these visitor. There is hardly any prostitution in the name of tourism as being circulated in a section of media. The American tourists are making a beeline for the Havana beaches and so are the Cubans to get a legal visa for the United States.

And the business is as usual. No one is hounding them to stay or to leave. Neither in the high seas nor in the air. In fact, he noticed dollar shops selling foreign goods in hard currency. According to Srivastava, it appears that American blockade is only in namesake to help the clandestine American businessmen to make an extra buck and that too without any competition.

Anti-Cubanism is a bogey in American politics to catch popular fancy against communism otherwise Cuba is evidently making necessary reforms in its economy to accommodate the fast increasing economic interest in this Caribbean island nation. It is high time the Indian business also wakes up to this changing scenario. There may have been some pitfalls when the situation was rather bad in Cuba and some Indian companies such as Cimmco might have had some unhappy experiences but the situation is changing fast and India should capitalise on it.

Coming back to the friendship societies, the Indian Society for Latin America (ISLA) launched in 1970s by the then Member of Lok Sabha Daulatsinhji P Jadeja (father of Ajay Jadeja) is also in a state of revival.

It has announced an ambitious function in April 1998 at Jamnagar in Saurashtra region of Gujarat to mark the fifth anniversary of Rio Earth Summit which took place in Rio de Janeiro and to launch an afforestation programme in the native coastal of the village of the Jadejas.

ISLA has invited all the ambassadors from the region for the occasion. Jadeja is credited with launching a one-man mission to promote Latin America in India through his influence in and out of Parliament during the 1970s and 80s.

The Russian and the Bindi

Kazakstan's fifth independence day celebrations recently marked a special point in Indo-Kazak relations. This oil rich Central Asian country has just given the license to India (ONGC) to explore oil in certain regions of the country which would eventually be placed at the disposal of India.

Even as three young Kazak girls attired in their traditional dress welcomed guests at the party (these girls are learning Kathak here), Kazakhstan's ambassador to India RT Ibraev talked about the improving relations with India.

While I was trying hard to resist the chocolate balls wrapped in golden foil that beckoned temptingly at the party, the Hon Consul of Nicaragua insisted that I taste the half a dollar each gold, foil chocolates! Of course my waning resistance gave away as the chocolate melted in my mouth wishing that there would be some half a dollar each mysterious eatable as well that would neutralise the fat I was consuming!

While I was guilty counting the calories, a Russian diplomat to whom I was introduced by a friend wanted to know the significance of my bindi throwing up a valley of questions. Questions that I have been asked numerous times.

Did married women put them? Did the colours signify anything? Did the shape signify anything? Did men put bindis, rather why they didn't? Why was my bindi a straight line and not round as seen on other women's forehead?

As I did my best to tell the diplomat that men did put tilaks since the ancient times although these days it is largely on religious occasions. Who can forget the shining sun on the forehead of Kama, or the very elaborate ones on the head of Indian kings, legendary heroes like Ram, Lakshman and so many others. In the South, men significantly used tilaks, both horizontal as well as vertical signifying the caste they belonged to. As for us, women it has become more decorative and more colourful and expensive day by day. I found myself thinking there should be a book published by some innovative publisher on the subject so that next time, I could refer him to the book.

Speaking of Indian women, it is very heartening to note the growing of DCWA (Delhi Commonwealth Women's Association) who work tirelessly from their office in Zamroodpur in a space donated by the Lt Governor of Delhi.

It began with the initiative of some Indian women who wanted to contribute to society and the wives of the diplomatic community were invited to participate. Today the wives of high commissioners of Commonwealth countries automatically become the honorary members while they are posted in India.

Since not many of the countries allow the wives to work while the husbands are in posting, many, of them wholeheartedly devote their time for the cause of the poor.

The DCWA's medical centre in Zamroodpur gives medicines to almost 100 patients every day free of cost. They also have a mobile medical van visiting the slums every week. They run a small nursery school with free cup of milk and bread with jam for the little students and even provide for operations and higher education to those who really need it.

The funds are collected through exhibitions, an annual ball and an international bazaar held in the lawns of Ashoka every year. Last year the wonder ladies raised Rs 27 lakh from the bazaar, this year they hope to raise more. They need more than a lakh to run the medical centre every month which has a full-fledged dental clinic, TB and cancer detecting centre. Yet they keep a low profile preferring to work on their own rather than apply for grants. The people of Zamroodpur and nearby areas have a lot to thank the members of the DCWA.

The Czech republic also celebrated their national day. It was the only one which was graced by the Indian Vice-President KR Narayanan. Czech ambassador to India Odolen Smekal speaks excellent Hindi, so much so that he can put to shame many of the Indians for whom our national language does not hold much importance as English. He has translated Premchand's Godan into Czech language and many of his native literature into Hindi.

A regular reader of *Navbharat Times*, Rajendra Awasthi is among one of his many favourite Hindi writers. The most interesting thing about him speaking Hindi is that there is only a faint trace of accent in his tone. "*Milte rahiye kabhi kabhie,*" he says as I proceed to leave.

One doesn't mean to sound prudish, but surely there are more important things to do, like some of us don't have water nor houses, and how about the Mosquitan invasion maa'm? Hey maa'm? Excuse me? Yoo hoo?

Last but not least, is someone who can't make up his mind whether Man-smart-woman-smarter safely sticking to being a bit of both! One speaks of Mikcy of the swinging, spiralling curls, and powered 25,000 apiece, with chowtime thrown in? -and... what?

Never mind where I got it from, and what? So the poor and the have-nots, besides, haven't you heard it's all in the name of charity?

Aapro Michael dikra ek pie pan nathi lidyo, translated, khali pili kaiko bom mart'a? Aapun ka Michael aisach hai, kya? Ek chavanni nakoch manta bidoo! Hail Jacko!

Role of Diplomats' Spouses in Foreign Land

It's a pure coincidence that I know both Algerian counsellor Abdelhamid Abdoui and his wife Laila who were involved in an unsavoury incident in Khan Market. At the same time I am also an avid reader of Sagarika's writings, especially on foreign affairs. The incident has been blown out of proportion, looming over our bilateral relations.

I do not remember much about Laila, fairly tall and well built, who chose to thrash *Outlook* journalist Sagarika Ghosh. I had met her very briefly when I visited the Algerian embassy to meet her husband Abdoul who is a soft-spoken, pleasant hardworking Arab diplomat from Sahara desert. He sounded genuinely concerned about promoting his country's image and creating goodwill in India. So was his namesake, ambassador Abdel Senouci Bereksi, with whom I have interacted half a dozen times in the last two years most of them at parties and diplomatic receptions. But I still remember the breakfast interview at his decorated bungalow at 23, Kautilya Marg, Chanakyapuri overlooking the vast span of greenery from his drawing room.

He was very emphatic about the role India can play in this part of the world and the traditional ties which the two countries have enjoyed with African countries in general and the sub-Sahara region in particular.

Unfortunately, Algeria has been hitting the headlines in India for not the best of the reasons. Continuing violence in that country unleashed by the fundamental forces against the well established secular credentials of the present dispensation, and now the Laila-Sagarika affair has brought bad publicity to Algeria.

I agree that the parking problem is assuming unmanageable proportions in the city due to the ever growing vehicular population. Incidentally, it was a holiday on Monday and there was enough space for parking in the busy Khan Market area.

But as it turned out to be, no one was willing to give way even an inch. What an irony that the affair involved India and Algeria who continue to vow in the tenets of non-alignment including peaceful co-existence.

It is indeed a pity that an ambassador should be summoned to express India's deep concern over misconduct of a subordinate's wife. Perhaps that's why the Indian Institute of Foreign Service produces a very apt and useful booklet on the role of diplomats' wives in improving the diplomatic relations between two countries. This booklet can certainly serve as a bible to all spouses. It goes in detail about the silent but effective contribution by the wives (in some cases the husbands as well) when the other spouse is at work.

There are umpteen number of cases where diplomats' wives mingle with the local people and generate much bonhomie for cementing the ties even in case of overtly hostile country such as Pakistan.

Here I am reminded of the wife of Pakistan's first secretary Afrasiab-Aasia. At a dinner at their house, I was pleasantly surprised to see mixing up with our homegrown Punjabi wives of Defence Colony like bosom chums. She had taken extra efforts to throw in a couple of vegetarian dishes keeping in mind the ongoing Navratri festival when many Indians choose to became vegetarian. A lot needs to be done in case of African countries which enjoy very cordial ties with India, albeit only at political level. Some measures must be adopted so that this relationship may percolate to the social level also.

Pardon me saying so, but I can understand an inbuilt resistance because of the colour prejudice in case of dark Africa. But that is not the case with white Africans of the Saharan region.

If the wives of the western diplomats can organise bazaars, fetes, auctions, exhibitions and charity work to come closer to India, why can't same work be done by the spouses from other missions from Asia and Africa.

In this regard, South Block can take a little more innovative approach and initiative in bringing the diplomatic families closer to the local populace.

Why did Vivan Stop Painting ?

There is a new arrival on the diplomatic scene in the Capital. The internationally acclaimed painter of India Vivan Sundrum, but he doesn't paint anymore.

I spotted him with Aroon Purie, the editor-publisher of *India Today* at the fund-raising Cuban evening at Taj Mansingh where his painting was bought by yet another newspaper baron Lalli (Lalit Mohan Thapar) and later sitting alone in a corner with his critic wife Geeta Kapoor.

In the blaring music and my hunger to taste Cuban delicacies, I somehow couldn't speak to him spotting him now and then chatting with guests. But its oil painting (the only one at the fund raising party) generated so much interest that I had to know more about him.

I believe more recently he surfaced in the Peruvian national day *vin d'honneur* held in the ball room of Park Royal which is fast becoming the latest rendezvous of diplomats and ex-patriates.

But at both the occasions, he was visibly ill at ease. The reason being, he is still remembered and invited as a painter while he is not one.

He is given to bigger things in life. He had left painting when it came under the auction hammer of Christie's and Sotheby. He was uncomfortable with the air-conditioned confines of the art galleries and the awe and terror they enthuse in the common man. Instead, he has joined hands with Sahmat of Safdar Hashmi fame where some like-minded friends and colleagues are trying to do something different in the field of arts.

On the 125th anniversary of Mahatma Gandhi, they had invited artists from the world over to do anything on the back of a post-card—something which was so dear to the Mahatma because he thought that was the best means of communication.

The art world had responded enthusiastically. According to a friend, now Vivan and his friends are in the process of celebrating the 50th year of Indian Independence through a five inch cube. They have invited painters and artists of other hues and shades to let their artistic creativity take fanciful flights on a five inch cube.

They expect 200 such cubes to arrive from so many countries which will be on display coming September. In fact, they have started arriving and are being preserved at the Vithal Bhai House on Rafi Marg.

The idea is to separate art and artist from the claustrophobic environs of formal and sophisticated socialites who have made this into yet another ladder of social climbing and money-making.

I am told Vivan has tried his hands at different things of this genre, like using the throw aways of a slum and converting them into exhibits on display in their own surroundings.

Recently, he was in Cuba where he met a lot of Latin American artists from Peru and Brazil who have promised to send their cubes.

That explains his presence at the Peru celebrations amidst former army chief K Sundarji of Bofors fame, P Murari who after relinquishing Rashtrapati Bhawan as the then secretary to former president Venkatraman has joined another president (of FICCI) as his adviser and of course the tall, slim and elegant lieutenant governor of Delhi Tejinder Khanna *sans* his matchingly graceful wife.

Lastly, a word about the tradition of *vin d'honneur.* For a few years now, we have been receiving invitations for one spouse (always the husband) for such parties. Pardon my ignorance and my inquisitive mind, but I have been wanting to know why it is only the husband? I was provided the answer only very recently.

According to an ambassador though a grand tradition, it is the best way to save a penny or two in the world of economising diplomatic initiatives.

Unlike evening receptions, you don't have to invite spouses in *vin d'honneur* which are necessarily held in the afternoons.

Though for Indian taste buds, they do serve harder liquors and some snacks, but it should be treated as wine tasting sessions!

Adding Colour to a Dull Meet

Venue: Napoleon Hall of five star hotel Le Meridien. Occasion: Prize distribution ceremony to leading Indian exporters by Israeli embassy. Chief guest: Going going gone Industries minister BB Ramaiah. Other guests: Leading industrialists and businessmen with a salt and pepper sprinkling of a few politicians and journalists. Incidentally I was one of them.

I would have quietly kept on listening to the speeches made by the Israeli ambassador, the Industries minister and other industrialists who were present to proudly receive the awards, sipped my fresh orange juice, gobbled on my dinner and walked out but for the activity that was going on the adjoining table. I could not help noticing an elegantly dressed middle-aged woman, gracefully graying with sparkling ornaments and well-anointed makeup. She stood out more because of her non-descript escort who happened to be a former Union minister. Indian politicians have been rather discreet about their private affairs in public. It has been reciprocated by the Indian media, barring exceptions such as Maneka Gandhi's journalistic forays when she chose to expose the clandestine activities of late Suresh Ram son of Cabinet minister late Jagjivan Ram. I also do not want to cross the Rubicon but what followed made an otherwise dull diplomatic party into a titillating affair.

Notwithstanding the august company, the woman was distributing her visiting cards in a non-chalant fashion not only on the table she was sharing, but even in the friendly neighbourhood. Let's just says the admirers were by now flocking to her—both young and old. Soon the entire neighbourhood had a choice between the dull and the mundane speeches delivered by the political leadership. She had the entire table eating out of her hands. The original escort—who by that time was adequately sozzled with generous helpings of scotch—could not take it any more.

In a style matching with medieval chivalry, he pounced on the table where he had lost his peace in floodlit ambience, caught her by the waist and guided her to the seclusion of his choice. The woman kept on saying, "O my bag and my cell..." But all her refrain fell on deaf ears and there went the couple-of-the-evening leaving the stunned audience with their whispering tones.

Coming to the main agenda of the evening, Israelis seem to have made deep inroads into the Indian corporate sector in almost every possible field.

They have set up joint ventures, made direct investments and are helping Indian products find their way to the newly-discovered market of the Middle East. The evening which was called in a "joint quest" had top corporate leadership of FICCI, CII, ASSOCHAM and PHDCCI.

The food served was typically Indian—ranging from *roghan josh* to *paneer kadai* and *dal makhani* to *ras malai.* According to the *Global*—an import export magazine by Srikand Khandekar which was given to all the guests at the reception—today there are more than 400 foreign companies which have set up facilities in Israel. Taking the total foreign investment to $2.5 billion in 1996.

Israelis have targeted the large Indian middle class. Today India accounts for 10 per cent of Israeli exports to Asia. However, the export basket of both the countries is limited to diamonds and chemicals.

Delhi-based companies including Sona Educational and Training Systems and VAM Organics and Chemicals Limited are collaborating with Israeli multinationals. India-Israel business alliance has been set up at FICCI to provide a single window solution to solve day-to-day problems.

Let me add here that the reception was in continuation with the celebration of the 50th year of Indian Independence which the Israelis have been doing with class as well as extravagance. Long live Indo-Israeli relations, which by the way are only five years old.

A Diplomatic Victory

While the world watched an emotional Chris Patten handing over Hong Kong, the Chinese celebrated its return to the motherland in as many ways as their imagination would allow; at least in India. First, they mounted a massive photo exhibition at Lalit Kala Gallery in Rabindra Bhavan coinciding with the arrival of their new cultural councillor Jiang Wei Ming then they invited a galaxy of Delhi-ites to show an hour-long film on the Chinese contribution to the present day development of their eight largest trading centres in the world which was followed by the specially commissioned film by Brig Chittaranjan Sawant An *eve on the dawn of Hong Kong* which was shown thrice on Doordarshan but the climax was the grand party in the Napoleon banquet hall of Le Meridien hosted by the Chinese Charge De' Affairs Zeng Xuyong who was at his polite best obliging the photo seekers and going out of his way to make his guests comfortable. Sawant's film told us that 28,000 odd Indians settled in Hong Kong out of which 22,000 still hold Indian passports are not overduly worried about the change of sovereignty in the island. Chinese have assured them and also the Indian government that like any other foreigner Indians will be allowed to contribute in the future development of Hong Kong.

Understandably Chinese joy knows no bounds in this hour of triumph and glory when they forced the sun to set in the eastern end of the British empire. History will always record that it was the Chinese who virtually brought an end to the two century old saga of British imperialism spanning over one-fifth of the globe from the far end of the western hemisphere to the east. Like the 18th day of the epic battle of *Mahabharata* today British crown has to contend with her few islands like Cayman. Bermuda and St Helena in an otherwise gem studded crown. Hong Kong was the last vestige of the European colonialism. There could not have been a more befitting tribute to this millennium which witnessed the subjugation of men by men, racial discrimination, economic slavery and cultural bondage.

Coming back to the party, our home grown communists, from Maulana Farukhi to Sitaram Yechuri and AB Burdhan, were in full attendance showing solidarity in the highest moment of rejoicing with their comrades-in-arms. But Chinese were not discriminatory in their invitations. BJP was represented by Brajesh Mishra, who had held the Indian consulate in Beijing when it was known as Peking. In fact a lot of credit goes to Mishra for breaking the ice across the Himalayas in Sino-Indian relations because of 1962. But it is not fashionable to talk about it now and let's not spoil the joyous mood of our 'regained' Chinese friends at the zenith of their diplomatic victory. Like the Convention Centre in Hong Kong the western diplomats were missing from the Napoleon party, to express solidarity with the British apprehensions that soon China might undo what British did in last 156 years.

However there were other distinguished Indian guests like the IIMC director JS Yadav who has been contributing to India diplomatic initiatives by hosting dozens of foreign student journalists every year. Besides Indians, China had other friends like the outgoing Iranian deputy chief of mission Naseer Saghafi—Ameri, his petite beautiful wife Gilehgol attired in smooth black complete with the black scarf held together with a pretty brooch and United Nations Information director Feodore Starcevik.

Gilehgol spoke in perfect though accented English opening the conversation with "nice to meet you". She looked at me pointedly while her husband burst into immediate 'dialogues' regarding international issues like the recent Algerian election, Hong Kong handover and other such topics.

Real party talk I told Gilehgol that one of my aunts had married an Iranian and always wore a "chador" whereby she exclaimed that she must be in some part of

Teheran because there the black cloak was called a "chador".

I added she had sons who spoke perfect Persian but couldn't understand a word of their mother's language. They had great difficulty communicating with their maternal grandmother who were visiting them.

"It largely depends on the mother, on how strong she it". Gilehgol told me. That one sentence shattered my image of Iranian women. Under that black cloak lurked women with determination. Dumbstruck, I headed towards the dinnertable making my way through beautiful Chinese women clad in shimmering silk and brocade gown slit to the thighs.

An array of Chinese delicacies consisting of Peking ducks, roasted pork, glugel steamed fish, the inevitable chowmein (authentic Chinese style this) and rice spread temptingly with salads and deserts on the table. As I filled my plate my eyes rested on a pot bellied laughing Buddha carved neatly on a pumpkin. Hands raised high and standing tall it looked as if it was joyously celebrating the moment too. Or perhaps, was it mocking my ignorance?

Oriental Features and Acceptance in Japan

There could not have been a better curtain raiser to the much-awaited Indo-Pak foreign secretary level talks than the ghazal evening at the Ashoka Hotel convention hall. Courtesy the audio cassette revolution, Ghulam Ali is a household name in India. In fact, now there is it tough competition among Pakistani singers to grab a slice from the Indian musical pie.

The manner in which Ghulam Ali conducted not only his accompanying musicians but the Indian audience made it impossible to believe the headlines screaming animosity between India and Pakistan. The audience clapped and cheered each time he sang his well-known ghazals. Culture has succeeded where diplomacy has failed. Indeed, it does seem that if we have to start building bridges across borders, we have to rely on unconventional modes ot communications. There is lot of goodwill between the peoples of the two countries, devoid of any initiated or inspired prejudices against each other, if Ghulam Ali could spin his numbers around the Hindustani ragas such as Aheer, Bhairavi and Malkauns, it is not difficult to decipher the imaginary lines which have divided us for last 15 years. As we enter the new millennium, we should pick up the threads from where previous generations left at some point of history.

When any Indian meets a Pakistani, say in Japan, he doesn't know-how to begin the fight because fight they will (must they?) as that's the way we have been brought up. My younger sister went on a scholarship to Osaka without knowing a word of Japanese.

Though our Oriental features do make us look like Japanese sometimes, more so in the case of my sister, the rigid Japanese society took a long time to make friendly overtures.

It was during this time that she met this wonderful Pakistani friend Shaheen settled in Japan who went out of her way to make her feel comfortable until she learnt enough Japanese to fend for herself. Having recently returned after spending a couple of years there, she does not yet tired of recollecting the wonderful time she had with her Pakistani friend. How does this come about in an alien land? It is the similar culture and deep friendship that bound the two in a foreign land.

The animosity that we have been brought up with towards each other vanishes under such circumstances. Now Shaheen is moving to Pakistan with her husband and has invited my sister to visit her there.

Would she he able to visit her without a mindset? Or if my sister invited her friend to India, would Shaheen be able to come without any preconceived notion. While writing this column, I am also reminded of a Pakistani Latin Americanist Ruksana Qausar who was all hunky dory till we were discussing the distant lands of Western hemisphere. The moment we came round to India and Pakistan, there was a sense of competition.

I remember fondly her desire to visit the dargah of Nizamuddin Aulia while we sat sampling food at the Karim's. With a sense of *deja vu,* I also followed her to the shrines which I had never done till then.

The Mughals ruled India for over 300 years. The British disintegrated their empire but also divided us for good. Not only geographically, but emotionally too. Whenever a family is divided between brothers, a sense of competition is inevitable. Historically, we were destined not to be equal but this fact is difficult to be reconciled with.

Then what is the solution? In-house competition could be a healthy corporate policy, but nothing could he more disastrous between estranged neighbours. This could only lead to mutual destruction. What else are we doing at the icy heights of Siachen or in the marshy lands of Gujarat or the deserts of Rajasthan? Let's not talk about Kashmir for the moment since it is fraught with sentimental journeys. But we can definitely buy peace on all other fronts spread over thousands of kilometres.

Be There!

If you want an indication of success, here it is: within five months of Being, the Pret Line clothing store launched by Gautam Singhania, CMD, Raymond Limited, at Shoppers Stop, Ansal Plaza, is now ready to expand. Four more sister stores in Mumbai, Ludhiana, Pune and in Karol Bagh are on the anvil. For years, designers cried themselves hoarse about the need for corporate backing, citing examples of the fashion industry in the West.

Nobody took them seriously, until Singhania stepped in. Now that he's tested the waters and come away successful, others are willing to take the plunge too. There are talks in the industry of Madura Garments and liquor baron Vijay Mallya getting into similar propositions.

The Ansal Plaza store came into existence targeting the local retail market with its Pret Line, affordable and wearable, with designer labels from Mumbai and Delhi.

The store's success, predictably, has vindicated the stand of fashion designers, though they admit it has been a learning process. They've had to work according to sizes and the store has had its share of merchandising problems. "We do need to store the merchandise according to the season and, at the moment, we do not stock woollens as such," says a store spokesperson. Not that this seems to have deterred consumers. The store has at least 400-500 customer walk-ins per day translate into good sales, though actual figures are not divulged. "Punjabis, Bengalis and Marwaris have been picking up these crinkled silk shirts by low profile Mumbai designer Priyadarshini Rao," point out the store manager.

"In fact, we've noticed that our rallies that are priced the least move the fastest", says the store manager. With BE's huge success, the industry is abuzz as to how it will spell the knell for other relatively smaller ventures without the muscle of corporate biggies. Says a designer on conditions of anonymity: "Places like Ogaan and Tarun Tahiliani are running secred". Still others claim how the same designers retailing from BE are getting picked up faster than from other smaller stores. Ogaan's Kavita Bhartia, however, argues: "Pret is still in its nascent stage and needs more organisation even though the numbers and quantity are there and it does reach a larger section of the consumers."

Bhartia points out: "The only stores which are doing well in the Pret a Porte category is Benetton. Even Next had to pull its shutters down," she adds.

5
First Hand Experience

Making their Diplomats Our Envoys: A User's Guide

The Indian Foreign Service is considered the sole repository of diplomatic initiatives and responses. Every year the ministry of external affairs brings out an annual report which contains such moves divided into various territorial divisions. But MEA does not function in vacuum. For every action taken by it, it has to depend on the other ministries of the Government of India. Hence it becomes the nodal agency to reach out to the world.

But almost every department of the government of India contributes substantially towards forging new alliances and strengthening the existing ones.

Let's take a few examples. It will be fair to begin with the various training programmes in almost every walk of life conducted by the autonomous or departmental institutes. The Foreign Service Institute (FSI) at Akbar Bhavan runs about half a dozen courses to train African, Asian and Latin American diplomats along with their Indian counterparts.

When these diplomats go back home to become ambassadors for their country, they carry an element of Indian ethos and a sense of gratitude for having been exposed to the subtle art of diplomacy. Neither Akbar Bhavan where these courses are held nor Lodhi Hotel where generally the foreign trainee diplomats are lodged are worthy of the functions bestowed upon them.

In fact, FSI is the only important outfit which doesn't have a building of its own. First the vacant plot diagonally opposite to Sonia Gandhi's residence was earmarked for MEA including this institute and later a matching piece of land was given on the old campus of Jawaharlal Nehru University but for reasons best known to MEA, nothing has come of it so far.

Unofficially, it is learnt that it doesn't fall under the priorities of the ministry. Each year a request is made in the budget allocation but it has not dawned on the people holding the purse strings that it would be more worthwhile to have the FSI building than many embassies abroad.

Frankly speaking, the MEA is the only ministry which is sandwiched between two heavyweights, namely the Prime Minister's Office and Defence with its offices scattered all over the place from Akbar Bhawan to Shastri Bhawan, Patiala House to Indian Society for International Law and Bhikaji Cama Place to Curzon Road.

Other offices can wait, but FSI which trains 100-odd foreign diplomats every year should not. It's in a way undoing whatever we are trying to achieve. There are many other well-known diplomatic training institutes in the so-called First World which attracts candidates from a lot of European and other developed countries. However, India has been able to establish its credentials in this sphere in the developing world. Lest this initiative is snatched away by others, we should act.

Incidentally the Indian Institute of Mass Communications, National Institute of Mass Communications, National Defence College, Oceanography Institute based in Goa, Kathak Kendra, National School of Drama, Film and Television Institute of India, National Defence Academy, Indian Defence

Akademi, Indian Management Institute, Lal Bahadur Shastri Academy of Administrators all have their own building and complexes. All of them likewise train foreign candidates as well. Even the thousands of African students studying in India with the scholarships offered by Indian Council for Cultural Relations (ICCR) go back impressed with the available infrastructure.

In fact providing professional and general education to foreign students is the other major area in which India has made diplomatic-strides. In the same context, the outgoing Kenyan ambassador, Terer was quoted in this column when he said that all the 8,000 students from there in India are the ambassadors of his country. I would like to add that they are ambassador of his country while being here but once they return they become our envoys because no one forgets his formative years and his alma mater.

Talking about education, this is an area which needs to be further explored. Under various educational agreements and Memoranda of Understanding (MoU) there is a provision for the exchange of pro-lessors for India Chairs in particular and otherwise in general. But sources in the University Grants Commission (UGC) confirm that more often than not, these vacancies go a begging. So do various scholarships offered by Indian and foreign governments on a reciprocal basis. The reasons are many but not difficult to understand. One is that the UGC makes no scholarships. There is a big nexus operating in the field of education which doesn't even allow genuine candidates to apply. One deserving case is of a Latin American scholar Dalbir Singh of JNU who despite close links with the then education State Minister Selja could not get hold of relevant information about half a dozen scholarships in that region.

Secondly, many countries have sent their teachers to be posted in Indian universities but all these agreements are on a reciprocal basis. If an Indian establishment is not willing to shell out its share of money, no solo tango can begin. There was a time when the world was full of Indologists who were spotted and cultivated by ICCR. But that species is fast becoming extinct and there is no visible effort to preserve or produce them afresh. The catchment area is easily decipherable. Does anyone have any record of the retired ambassadors posted some time or the other in New Delhi. These former envoys can easily double up as India hands. During my trips with the President and Prime Minister, I did not notice any former ambassador of the host country invited to the umpteen receptions held in honour of the visiting Indian dignitaries.

The Government of India and private institutions spend a fortune in training Indian students in foreign languages. The School of languages of JNU is a case in point. Barring a few enterprising pass outs who end up as teachers or tourist guides, most of these foreign linguists of sorts go waste. UGC has never thought of creating slots for the thousands of students passing out of the area study centres and language schools. Our corporate sector needs people well versed in languages of the countries they deal with. But there is no mechanism where the horse could be led to the well. There is no dearth of Indian initiatives and responses but this has to be taken to its logical conclusion in order to extract maximum mileage.

Sri Lanka Sends One Man Army to Catch Indian Travellers

If the legend of Rama is be believed, India has been sending its army to Sri Lanka—sometimes to crush the devil king Ravana or at times to restore peace in the northern province of Jafna. This time it is the Sri Lankans who have sent a one man army—neither to avenge an insult nor to crush a rebellion. It is to capture and conquer the rich and the willing Indian traveller to the lure of virgin beaches, the affordable hospitality and the excellent corporate unwinding facilities.

This one man army is manned and commanded by the soft spoken suave and sober Panisene Viratne who starts blushing whenever he sees his name in print instead of Ceylon Tourism Board whom he represents in India.

The brief of Sene Viratne is travel and tourism diplomacy. And he has an impeccable record to perform and encore. Before being sent to India, he was invited by the Grenada government in central Amenca to define, shape and mould the tourism policy.

Indian tour operators can learn a lesson or two from the way Sri Lankans have gone about in converting a strife torn, nation into a popular tourism destination. Sri Lanka has emerged strong not only from the adjoining south Asian nations but also far flung Germany, France and even India.

They have sun, sea and Buddha. So have we. That's different matter that our great Hindu revivelist Adi Shankaracharya sent Buddhism packing to Cambodia. Tailand and Japan, Vietnam, Mongolia and Laos. But the Buddhist believers the world over continue to return to the motherland of the lord, be it Kapilavastu, Gaya, Sravasti, Sarnath and the likes. It is shocking but true that ambassadors from a dozen Buddhist countries have joined hand in an effort to resurrect the Buddhist circuit in India. In fact, they are in a continues state of daze that India allowed this great heritage to shatter into ruins. This group, headed by the well meaning Sri Lankan high commissioner in India, Mangala Moonersing, made the beginning by requesting the government of India to renovate the Buddhist guest house outside New Delhi's railway station.

When India's former minister of state for external affairs, Jalman Khurshid adopted his father's constituency (Farukkhabad) to come to Lok Sabha, his priority list was headed by a grand plan to connect the Buddhist shrine at Farukkhabad, Sardsa to the national circuit. He was amazed to find so many takers for the project. It is high time the India Tourism Development Corporation (ITDC) adopted the Buddhist circuit as a top priority destination. This is because after the fly by night shoppers, it is the Buddha followers who form the largest group of international travellers.

According to Seneviratne, Sri Lanka has no Taj Mahal or Konark. It is also not endowed with such an abundance of jungles, deserts and mountains like India has. But it asked its people to open their doors to the foreign guests and they converted one room each in their homes as budget tourist accommodations. It was in early 1980s when LTTE tigers had not surfaced and the country had just been converted into a duty free port. The result was the arrival of 94,000 tourists.

LTTE reducted it to half in the next decate, but the last four years have exploded the myth of Sri Lankan vulnerability. This year they are expecting 50,000 foreign tourists and another 10,000 extra in the next. Seneviratne is confident that he could convert Sri Lanka into a major catchment area. While talking to him, one fell the great potential of SAARC regional tourism. The tourism promotional agencies of the region could easily sell a combined packet to Europe and the rest. The combined packet could extend from the Himalayan kingdoms of Bhutan and Nepal to the Indian ocean pearls of Sri Lanka and Maldives with Indian sub-continent in between. This idea has been floated and discussed threadbare in successive SATTE (South Asia Travel and Tourism Exchange) conferences.

Sri Lankan tourism diplomacy is ably supported by Air Lanka which has connected Colombo with Delhi,

Mumbai, Chennai, Thiruvanathapuram and Tiruchiraplly. But the policy planners international civil aviation in India continue to put spokes in every bilateral diplomatic spanner. Like many other international airlines they also allow Air Lanka to up only 3,500 passenger every week while there is a potential for 5,000. Not that Indian Airlines is able to take advantage of this but this dog in the manger policy is leading us no where.

Political leadership in successive dispensations have been convinced by the bureaucrats in Jawahar Bhawan that India should not give away its optimum capacity on a platter. Air Lanka has been pressing to be allowed to connect pava and Bangalore in its circuit. The seven-year-old airlines will soon be adding a business class and group fare for Indian travellers.

Indian public sector may be sleeping on its out of use laurels but leading hotel chains like Taj and Oberoi have woken to this new dawned reality.

Taj Samudra which has been rebuilt on the famous Colombo club now appears to be rising out of 11 acres of landscaped gardens and facing the historic Galle Face Green on the water front. Similarly the 500 room Lanka Oberoi was recently reborn on the main coastal thoroughfare of Colombo. What Sri Lankans are trying to achieve in India, if it could be reciprocated by the host country and other nations of the region, then the non-starter SAARC may come alive through sources other than diplomatic.

The Nicaraguan Lesson

Yesterday, an inconspicuous news item in *The Asian Age* datelined Nicaraguan capital Managua caught my fancy. The three paragraph notes stuff in Asia revealed less, concealed more. The item was regarding Nicaraguan president Arnoldo Aleman's visit to Taiwan in August. It is quite usual for a head of state to visit another country even if it meant crossing the Pacific and Indian Ocean or the other way around, across Atlantic as was this case.

It reminded me of a chance meeting with ambassador Salvador E Stadthagen of Nicaragua to Taiwan who had come here to represent his country during the ministerial meeting of the Non-Aligned.

He had told me of the great potential his country has for any one willing to take notice and advantage of. And how Taiwan continues to he referred to by the age-old name Republic of China in their bilateral parlance availed the same. After the US and Canada, Taiwan is one of the biggest investors in Nicaragua. It employs more than 8,000 locals in the business outfits it runs there. Obviously there are virtually little relations with the mainland China, or Hong Kong for that matter, except trade through third countries such as Panama. No wonder, on the eve of the visit of president Almeno, Taiwan declared a further grant of US $ 180 million to Central American and Caribbean allies in Central America.

Later I learnt that the eight countries of Central American region with which India has minimal contacts—Guatemala, Honduras, El Salvador, Nicaragua, Costa Rica, Panama, Belize and Dominica—have become the diplomatic battleground for recognition between China and Taiwan. It all started when Sino-US relations were colder than the cold war with the Soviet block. During that period many of these Central American nations embarked on a pragmatic course which ambassador Stadthagen described as engaging diplomacy, by wooing two pariahs, namely Taiwan and Israel, who were historically identified with the American lobby. The gamble continues to pay rich dividends except some marginal loss of face like not getting the full membership of Non-Alignment Movement. President Aleman's visit is a natural corollary to that gambit initiated in the cold war era. At that time it was not only unfashionable but highly dangerous if anybody pursued any link with Taiwan or Israel.

Our own home-grown Taiwan supporter, Ram Swarup, had to spend many years in jail because of writing letters to the editor and sponsoring trips to Taipei for Indian journalists and politicians. It's a different story that later he was released with full honours. But by that time 'Hindi Chini bhai bhai' had not returned to the Indian winds and Indian businessmen had started third country trade with Taiwan to such an extent that the South Block had to give permission for a Taiwanese trade mission in Vasant Vihar and a few independent trading houses operating from Samrat Hotel.

Coming back to Stadthagen's revelations, land was still available is his country for a song—Rs 1,000 per square metre for any thing; any foreign investor wants. Maybe for starting a hotel, Garment production and its exports, pharmaceuticals were other such areas where Indians could make their money.

The honorary consul of Nicaragua in India, Vivek Burman of Dabur, has another glamorous idea up his sleeves. He wants his friends from Bollywood to go and shoot Hindi films in the picturesque Nicaragua, the largest nation in the region; sparsely populated and hence mostly virgin. Its a green bridge joining the two large Americas together. Crossroads of different visions, cultures and dialects, where civilisations of great and remote splendour were trapped by the silence of stone, and where men of white complexion mixed their blood with theirs.

The green and fertile land dotted by mountains and volcanoes, blue sea and colour so intense it makes your eyes and soul fly. After an eight hour flight from London to Miami, it is another two hours away.

India and Nicaragua had severed their diplomatic ties at the turn of this decade after Sandinistas were wiped out in the general elections. But it is also a fact that India had put all its eggs in the Sandinista basket. Burman's appointment is a right step in the direction which could pave the future course.

Now when comparative studies are being done between Somoza's dynastic rule and Sandinista regime, literal skeletons are coming out of the clandestine graves of the latter period. However the lessons of the engaging diplomacy of Nicaragua and other Central Asian countries are loud and clear. India may continue to host 100-odd embassies here and maintain a matching number abroad, but it must identify its regions and countries of priorities. Gujral doctrine is fine but the world doesn't end there. Under this doctrine we have already committed to give more than to take. But the point is, we have to find a competitive market for our goods, profitable ventures for investment and lucrative ventures for joint collaborations, all this can't be found in our neighbourhood. Even America adheres to the Monroe doctrine of protecting Latin America like its backyard but it has not stopped it from doing business with Japan and China.

Our indulgence in our neighbours is more than welcome to maintain peace at our doorstep but after peace, what? That is where India has to look east and westwards. Our global concern for South-South dialogue through platforms like G-15 has refused to take-off. Even movements like Non-Alignment are getting feeble and ineffective. Now is the time when India should select countries companies and persons for a targetted approach.

There are four honorary consuls representing central American countries namely Nicaragua, Belize, Costa Rica and Granada. The four can join hands to take a joint initiative. When I cheeked out with Belize's Mohinder Singh Sahni, he was more than willing. Hope others agree with him.

Rotterdam, Gateway to Europe-92

The New Dutch ambassador to India, H J du Marchie Sarvass, has a definite mission apart from his routine chores—to identify Dutch roots in India. Sarvass believes that Dutch traders in the 17th century settled on the coasts of Cochin, Surat and Chinsua near Chandranagar in West Bengal. He says that the remains of their habitations which include churches, houses and graveyards—can throw a lot of light on Indo-Dutch cooperation. He plans to resurrect them in the form of monuments.

His predecessor Eegje Schwo, a non-career diplomat, developed a deep interest in Indian paintings during her tenure and carried off scores of works by various celebrated artists. Before her departure late last year, the National Gallery of Modern Arts exhibited her collection.

Now settled in Amsterdam she intends to set up a permanent Indian exhibition. She wants to pursue her passion and for that purpose has kept a place in New Delhi also.

Sarvass, when approached by *The Independent* for an interview, was busy preparing for the Dutch national day celebrations on April 30, which happens to be Queen Beatrix's birthday.

Dwelling on Indo-Dutch collaboration in trade and industry, tourism and culture, Sarvass regretted India's restrictions on foreign investors and those desiring to set up joint projects.

No wonder Dutch interest in India has shown a downward trend. He gave a specific example of India not showing sufficient interest in the prospect of 12 European countries coming together in 1992. Rotterdam, the biggest sea port in the world, will be the gateway to Europe for any country to send its goods. Though many other Asian countries have set up outfits there to take advantage of the port's role as a distribution centre, India seems to be oblivious: to dealing with 320 million people from one window.

Coming back to cultural ties, the ambassador said that after the independence of Surinam a large number of people of Indian origin opted to settle down in his country. Today they form an integral part of Dutch society, to which they are contributing in many ways. In a passing reference he mentioned the Sikhs, who at times took advantage of the liberal Dutch laws to voice their opinion about Khalistan.

Dutch scholars have shown a deep interest in the study of ancient India and indology. The Arya Samaj has sent many preachers to the Netherlands to spread their thought among both the old settlers and the new immigrants. In fact immigration after 1975 can easily be described as the largest since 1873 when Indians from Uttar Pradesh left as indentured labourers.

Talking about South Africa, Sarvass said there is virtually no link between the present white rulers of Dutch origin in South Africa and the Dutch back home in Holland. In fact the Hague has always opposed apartheid and considers South Africa just another country which failed to heed world opinion. But now things are changing.

The Dutch envoy expressed surprise that India had not done enough to attract foreign tourists from his country even in the 'Visit India Year' compared to other Asian countries like Singapore and Indonesia. The latest figures he had were for 1988 when only 28,000 tourists from his country visited India. After coming here he realised that events in Punjab, and Jammu and Kashmir have no impact on the rest of the country as far as tourism is concerned. But people abroad are afraid to come to India because of the wrong impression that the atmosphere here is bad.

6
Journal

Cultivating Relations with Nations Through Ambassadors

The departure of an ambassador after the successful completion of his tenure in the host country is a poignant moment. Apart from the assessment by the peers in his foreign ministry and the watchers of his country elsewhere, he himself is bound to get into a reflective mood over his own performance. Chilean ambassador Uldaricio Figueroa Pla (1993-97) is renowned expert on international organisations. He has two exhaustive volumes on international organisations and a manual to his credit. That apart, he is also known for his work on Bolivian maritime. During his stint President Shankar Dayal Sharma visited Chile. Indian exports to his country rose from US $ 5 million to $ 60 million. The imports went up from $ 1.5 million to $ 85 million, no mean achievement by any standards. He has laid the foundations for bio-technological and genetic exchange and setting up a centre for Indian studies in Chile.

However, an ambassadorial stint is a short span in diplomatic continuum. The incumbent picks up the thread left by his predecessor, carries it to the best of his ability within the strict confines of national brief and limiting conditions obtained in the country of his posting. His success depends on multiple factors such as the priorities of the two countries concerned vis-a-vis each other as well as the political will of the respective leaderships. The task becomes more challenging when it comes to a remote county and a far flung hemisphere figuring in the traditional mould of diplomatic preferences. Indo-Chilean relation is a case in point.

Despite a plethora of popular goodwill on either side, there is telling apathy for taking any bold-initiative. India boasts of hosting 129 resident embassies but do majority of them figure in is diplomatic, political and economic considerations. Does our political leadership find time to sit with them individually to share common perceptions about out lofty ambitions such as the Non-Aligned Movement and south-south dialogues. South Block apologists would shrug and ask is it humanly possible to cultivate so many ambassadors at the same time.

Agreed, there are territorial divisions to dust the bilateral relations periodically but that does not set the pace. There are occasional bilateral visits even at the highest level which do result in joint communiques, MoUs, cultural exchanges, academic and business conferences.

But that does not satisfy an enthusiastic ambassador who comes with the great hope of giving new directions to the relationship between his country and the host.

More often than not it does not happen. Ambassadors come and go. Even the quantum of bilateral trade also keeps on shooting. But believe me that will happen, notwithstanding the diplomatic fanfare because that is now governed by market forces in the domain of private enterprise. For example, out of the $ 60 million Chilean exports, 75 per cent was on account of copper alone and that is done by periodical meetings between Hindustan Copper and its Chilean counterparts in Mumbai and Santiago.

1 am not trying to undermine the importance of diplomatic initiatives in increasing the business. In fact, Chilean ambassador was all praise for his Indian counterpart Ram Mohan an old Latin America hand in South Block for the upward swing in the bilateral relations ever since he was posted there. But that is not enough. I will illustrate this by another example.

I had accompanied President Sharma to Chile in 1995. As it happens, the guest invited the host President to India who promptly accepted the offer and grand plans were announced to create the right kind of atmosphere prior to his visit through Chilean films on Indian television and foreign ministerial level meetings to set the tone and agenda for summit. President's secretariat dutifully reported the enthusiasm to Prime Minister's office and period. Nothing happened till date.

It sounds great but are we geared to fully exploit the occasion for pushing the bilateral relations in the right direction. Or will this visit also go the way Brazilian president Cardoso's went. He had also come with an unprecedented large contingent of businessmen to establish trade ties with India but like similar visits that too ended in exploratory exercises. Columbians had discovered Latin America by chance while setting out to find India five centuries ago. How long will India and Latin America keep on rediscovering each other? In fact the problem is we have not recovered from North America and Euro-centric diplomacy which is legacy of our colonial past.

Indian foreign ministry has one complete division for three countries: the US, Canada and the Bahamas, two divisions for Europe while 46 countries of Latin America is the additional charge of a joint secretary. Out of which we have full-fledged diplomatic missions only in 143 countries. Not long ago, Latin America was a part of the American division. Air India doesn't go below Chicago. India Tourism Development Corporation (ITDC) does not have an office beyond New York. Indian council for cultural relations keeps on sending Kathak dancers and sitar players to that part of the whole world but has it counted the Indologists in Latin America universities and autonomous centres.

There is a wide interest about India in those countries. Yoga and Indian spiritualism attract the largest number of tourists from that region but our secularism doesn't allow us to have a Hindu Circuit (through Buddhist circuit is a part of our itinerary). There is no mechanism to keep a track of former ambassadors to India who could double up as our friends at large. ICCR must divert its funds to build on India watchers rather than an occasional exposure of our performing arts which make little sense to an uninitiated audience.

Frankly speaking, we forget 100-odd ambassadors (apart from the dollars and Euro currency envoys) after giving them a four-horse carriage ride in the courtyard Rashtrapati Bhawan of at the time of presenting the credentials and then remembering them only for a farewell before his departure. The interregnum three-four years, they keep on waiting for audience from the Raisina Hills.

Ticklish Issues and an Ambassador at Large

There is a subtle diplomacy being practised by the honorary councils of various countries in India who happen to be successful businessmen. Like in the ease of Vivek Burman, who represents Nicaragua in this category of envoys and is also the managing director of Dabur group of companies. Nicaragua is one of the largest states of central America and very sparsely populated.

Burman is as popular in the diplomatic circle as perhaps his products are in the country. He hosted the last monthly lunch for the deputy heads of mission and minister counsellors recently. Usually there is always somebody from the South Block who attends these meetings. It was the Director, Passports and Visas, Ms Saha this time.

Unlike the usual get together at cocktails and national day parties where the crowd is so large that you can just manage only a nod even to the most familiar ones, there is direct interaction among the diplomats – both Indian and foreign leading to useful exchange of information in such meetings.

In this case a question-answer session at the end of the lunch dealt with visas for dependents, foreign prisoners in different prisons across the country wanting to change or waiting deportation etc. formed the most interesting part of the informal lunch. All the questions were answered patiently by the Director, Passport and Visa who many-a-times had to remind the diplomats that India is a very big country and has its own regulations. Especially in the case of foreign criminals which involves the police as well.

On many occasions recognising the nationality of the criminal itself was a huge problems. What do you do if you are just sent an audio cassette of the criminal from some part of the country requesting you to identify the nationality of the person? Well, here's a real diplomatic problem!

While many diplomats posted here write about their stint in India without of course failing to mention, about the popular Pushkar mela in Rajasthan (it is a must in almost every diplomat's itinery), there is one ambassador who has churned out a book on his country.

Somalian ambassador Mohammed Osman Omar's second book on the ethnic war raging in Somalia tilled *Somalia: A Nation driven to Despair* is a personal account of records and events that has taken place in his country. At time he reflects sadly on these events and at times angrily. His first book *The Road to Zero, Somalia's Seif*

Destruction was a reasonable success, most of which was written when the civil war was on in Somalia. He writes easily with a lucid flow. His book is a painstaking account of the western forces who are trying to impose their own model of democracy on his ethnically strife torn country. With virtually no government in his country, Mohammed is an ambassador-at-large trying to keep the moral of his fellow countrymen high, not only in India but in all parts of the world. He is one of the most active ambassador in New Delhi dividing his time between lawn tennis, seminars and cocktails despite being a teetotaler.

Ambassador Mohammed is a man of many talents, writing being just one of them. Though, when and how he gets the time to write despite his busy schedule is a mystery. And then again he could a teach a thing or two to budding chefs, his pastas and lasagnas (he makes the flat noodles himself) are mouthwatering and his pizzas are out of this world.

I still remember when I couldn't make it to his house one particular evening he had sent me the delicious pizza all packed and full of cheese. When I met him next he was showing me the bottled lime and chilly pickles stacked neatly in his kitchen shelf. "They are for some my lady ambassador friends," he said. Somalia is not an exception when it comes to countries with disputed status back home. Sahrawi Republic is another example of a embassy without a formal ambassador and a government. Despite rooftop sympathetic proclamations by successive governments.

New Delhi is yet to send the agreement for the acceptance of a ambassador of Sahrawi. Surprisingly enough leaders like Gujral Indrajit Gupta and Surjeet were in the vanguard of Indian support to Sahrawi's request for a full-fledged ambassador when they were in opposition. It is obvious that the South Block mandarins call the shots when it comes to ticklish diplomatic issue. Here the deterrent factor being the Moroccan opposition in particular and the division of OIC members in general over the status of Sahrawi.

Another example "is Taiwan which has been allowed to open trade mission in Vasant Vihar despite no formal diplomatic relation between the two countries. Gone are the days when India was in dilemma over Chinese Achilles heels like Taiwan and Tibet. Today India is maintaining a respectable distance and a formidable posture with all parties concerned.

Welcome on Board, Homai Saha

It was an eventful for the Indian Latin Americanists which marked the departure of a popular ambassador from Colombia Carmenza Jaramillo and the arrival of a new joint secretary Homai Saha to head the Latin American division in the ministry of External Affairs.

To the best of my memory, she is the first woman to head this division and who has succeeded her husband Debbrata Saha. She brings with her rich and varied experience in diplomacy ranging from external publicity to passport and visa division apart from a couple of postings abroad. When I met her last year in her Patiala House office, I had noticed her sharp perception and clear thoughts on the ticklish issues related to foreign travel—something so close to every Indian heart.

Saha has taken the charge of this rather low profile division at a very opportune time when our relations with the region as a whole and with respective countries are on an unprecedented swing.

We have had top level visits from president Cardoso of Brazil, president Fujimori from Peru, prime minister Panday from Trinidad and Tobago in a last year-and-a-half and the visits of president Menem of Argentina and president Frei from Chile are on the anvil.

Ministry of Commerce has embarked upon a very ambitious course to cross US $ 1,000 million mark in the exports. For this purpose they have asked the Federation of Indian Chambers of Commerce and Industries (FICCI) to set up an Indo-Latin American interest group comprising Indian businessmen dealing with the region, officials of various ministries and media persons to create awareness about Indian products and to facilitate linkage through air and shipping and by making structural changes in custom duties.

When Chidambaram was the commerce minister in the Rao government, he had asked the India trade promotion organisation (ITPO) to help Indian exporters participate in Latin American fairs and vice versa.

Since then, the ITPO has been publishing the only bilingual trade journal *Pragati India* in English and Spanish to bridge the communication and information gaps between the two regions.

There are sufficient shipping linkages now to reduce the time and freight factors to reach South America but the direct air link is still elusive. The only hope that the direct flight to South Africa would come handy was belied after a rather poor response even to South Africa.

Till that doesn't happen, the mental barrier has to be surmounted because if we can travel upto western hemisphere in the North, why can't we undertake a connecting journey towards the South. Those who have done it are keeping the results and the consequent profits close to their hearts lest they might have to share.

In fact there are so many success stories like Nancy Crafts who have created niche markets in Latin American countries in areas including garments through sheer perseverance and hardwork.

The need of the hour is to make our products known through participating in their fairs, sending commercial counsellors to all the 13 Indian embassies in Latin

America, setting up permanent brochure and product profile exhibitions, inviting their businessmen for familiarisation trips and cultivating trade journalists. Frankly speaking, till we don't open embassies in all the 33 countries, we can easily do with an institution called honorary consuls. For this purpose businessmen with proven credentials should be approached as have been done by Nicaragua, Costa Rica, Belize and Granada in the last two years. We should encourage other countries also from the Caribbean, Central America and the main continent.

It is high time we also look at the 13 political entities called dependencies or allied countries still attached to the Netherlands, Britain, France and the US. There is a lot of scope for attracting their tourists to India.

But unfortunately, neither Air India nor India tourism development corporation (ITDC) look below the Miami sector. A couple of years ago, ITDC participated in the Madrid fair of tour operators from Latin America (COTAL) and won the best stall award. But that is history now. Sita Travels had entered an agreement with COTAL to represent its members' interest in India, but one didn't hear much on that front.

Talking about Caribbean reminds us of 1.5 million people of Indian origin settled in Guyana, Trinidad, Surinam and Jamaica. We don't seem to be sure what to do with them. Some time, we talk about bringing them back to their roots, sometime making them culturally more Indians than what we are and at other times teaching them Hindi, sitar and Bharatnatyam.

Whatever we do, that should be on a long term basis and without disturbing the fragile balance they maintain with the people of African origin in the multicultural society and turbulent polity.

I have been told that the Royal Caribbean cruises have become very popular among adventurous Indian travellers. I wish if the self-style culture wallahs are taken on those cruises to apprise them that the days of Bhojpuri and Bihar 150 years ago are gone with the winds and these people are not Indian in that sense of the word, there is an exodus among them, it is towards the north and not towards East India—as they prefer to call us. However culturally it is a captive constituency for us and we should communicate with them culturally without insisting on linguistic prejudices.

As far as culture is concerned, the whole of Latin America can be our catchment area. Recently there was an impromptu poll in one of the prisons of Venezuela. The inmates were asked to name the 10 Indian they knew. Most of them started in the order of Gandhi and Sai Baba. The latter is equally popular in all most all the countries.

And so are yoga and brahmkumaris. All these factors account for a large number of tourist. If we can talk about a Buddhist tourist circuit, why can't we develop a spiritual circuit. After all, we are talking about market economy and globalisation.

In a more serious vein, Indian culture has attracted Latinos since the days of Tagore. Our Sahitya Akademi and the Spanish school of JNU continue to translate and interpret Marquaisc, Llosa and Borges why can't we translate our best literature in their language. *Papeles da la India*—the Spanish literary and cultural journal of Indian council for cultural relations (ICCR) should concentrate more on Indian literature rather than critiques and treatises.

Finally, the Latin American programme of School of International Studies has been churning out MAs, M Phils and PhDs in Latin America since last 20 years but our education system or our corporate sector has no use of them. Let the MEA, UGC and FICCI sit together to create a two-way traffic between business academia and diplomacy—Saha will look into it.

Kenya has 8,000 Ambassadors in India

I have not seen it in any other diplomatic mission. Students in the lobby, in the courtyard, outside the premises. The Kenyan High Commission is always bubbling with its students waiting for a paper to be signed, scholarship to be collected, message to be sent to Nairobi or to glance through a local newspaper from back home. The High Commissioner JK Terer calls them his country's 8,000 ambassadors in India. They are his primary concern. He wants them to be professionally trained here so that they could serve the motherland better. He wants their education curriculum hereto be institutionalized at the tertiary level. Talking during his instinct stint in India, columnist about his two years stay in India in the week preceding his National Day (Dec 12), he dealt at length about his world view which, at times, sounded unconventional, but convincing. He wants the word non-resident to be removed from our vocabulary. Kenya has 70,000 people of Indian origin, mainly from Gujarat, Maharashtra and Punjab, the noted film journalist of United News of India, BB Nagpal, is one of those whose family decided to come back to their roots some decades ago. Terer doesn't want them to be known as Indians, non-resident Indians or even of Indian origin. They are Kenyans Period. He reminded of Jawaharlal Nehru who had said in early 50s. While talking to some non-resident Indian abroad, "Stop looking back towards New Delhi at every drop of a hat. Belong to the place you have chosen to live and work. Contribute to the growth of the adopted land."

Alas! South Block has forgotten the sane advice given by the architect of the modern Indian foreign policy.

Whenever an African Kenyan applies for an Indian visa, he gets it for 21 days. But when an Indian Kenyan applies, he gets it for five years with multiple entry facility. I feel this discrimination is outright bizarre and should be stopped henceforth.

This is not the only discrepancy in the perception of India's foreign office. Kenya is one of those countries who has been allotted a piece of land in Chanakyapuri to build US mission, but New Delhi is asking for a market price which is exorbitant even by modest standards. India had allowed similar piece of land for a nominal price to all those missions who were willing to reciprocate the gesture. This can't happen in Nairobi because India had already built its chancery during the British days. There is an urgent need to review India's policy towards the allotment of land in New Delhi. We spent millions of rupees on bilateral relations in organising 'made in India' shows, film festivals, visits of dignitaries and artists. Can't we make one time gesture of giving a suitable piece of land somewhere else in Delhi, if not in Chanakyapuri.

That reminds me of Burkina Faso where the then Prime Minister PV Narasimha Rao had gone last year and chose to announce the Kashmir elections from its capital, Ouagadougou. He had even formally opened Indian mission there. That small country has reciprocated the gesture by coming to New Delhi but with no premises in mind. They are camping in hotel Le Meridien waiting for a suitable place. If government of India can find space for its ever proliferating non-descript offices, why cant't it have a provision for such exigencies. After all, countries are not multiplying at the rate of Indian bureaucracy.

I agree with High Commissioner Terer when he said: "priority is function of modern diplomacy". He was replying to a question about the lack of exposure to African culture in India. He started by saying if the choice was between a new mission in a country of vital importance and a cultural centre in an existing mission, the choice would not be difficult to make. However, he hastened to add that Kenyans have done their bit on the cultural score.

In the recently held Commonwealth Women's Association's annual mela on the lawns of Ashoka Hotel, Kenyan women dispatched its garments and handicrafts. By the end of the day, they went laughing to the bank. On every Africa day, Kenyan students put up endless shows singing and dancing. The same is the case with the shows organised by ICCR. Having said this, he took a discomforting pause and added, "Asians are perhaps not aware of the cultural, religious and linguistic vacuum created by the foreign rulers in Africa which is not the case with India or other countries of this region. A whole generation is struggling to find its roots. That is why we have to make an extra effort to find our idiom back and to speak to the world in our forgotten languages and to express ourselves through our ethos.

Former Ambassadors Flocking to Delhi

I was in two minds about accepting an invitation for a party thrown by Captain SP Singh, hosted in the fond memory of his late father and renewed journalist DN Singh. It was a painful coincidence: Both these personalities were consigned to flames on the same day and in the same crematorium. One will always remember SP Singh for his impeccable presentation of *Aaj Tak* in a language that the masses could identify easily. I am told that both of them belonged to the same region of eastern UP bordering Bihar, though there was a gap of a generation.

I did not know DN Singh, but if so many people could turn up for the evening I am sure there had to be an extra-ordinary magnetism, or perhaps it was just the human touch in the personality of this man who could inspire so many journalists.

Also, I felt it was a noble thought on part of the bereaved son to collect all those all who were associated with his father. The gathering included former Indian ambassadors IP Singh and Ramesh Arora, both of them have joined Bharatiya Janata Party to augment its foreign policy formulations, editor-turned-politician KR Malkani, current editors like Shekhar Gupta and Pushp Shraf and almost a whole generation of retired and serving journalists who had the privilege of working with the highly respected stalwart—DN Singh.

Had I not attended the party, I would have never come to know that the species called 'former Indian diplomats' are mushrooming in the Capital. We already have a galaxy of former foreign secretaries Salman Haider, JN Dixit, SK Singh, Muchkund Dubey, AP Venkateshwaran and MK Rasgotra. All of them are gainfully busy in presiding over seminars, writing columns, participating in radio and television discussions and trotting the globe—courtesy their former contacts and present patrons.

The manner in which these former diplomats are doing their political preferences in public, shows that Indian bureaucracy is not really that a political as it appears. Secondly, political parties are injecting some professionalism in their ranks.

With the 50th anniversary of India's Independence round the corner, the theme of discussion veered around India's freedom struggle; the concept of patriotism; nationalism, and the role of Nehru and Gandhi. It was shocking to note how our universally acclaimed national leaders were kept in abysmally low esteem by the BJP ideologues. I was told that according to BJP foreign policy think-tank, Gandhi's world-view was limited despite a long political apprenticeship in South Africa, and Nehru's vision was eclipsed by self aggrandisement. They think Gandhi was naive and Nehru was patronising. One of them wants to write a chronological account of the political murders. I was wondering what all happened to the so-called national consensus on India's foreign policy if its main protagonists differed with the founding fathers of India's international relations, and how could its protagonists execute the policies while in office.

But wait—there was a silver lining in the fast changing political alignments and the bureaucracy was also correspondingly crystallising.

Anyway, back to the party. I am sure DN Singh would have been happy to know that the party given in his fond remembrance had exactly the same topics that he as a journalist would have loved to discuss himself.

7
In the End It's the Word

Chamber Diplomacy

Ever since India ushered in the liberalised economy to compete in the global free market trade, the traditional diplomacy has given way to various chambers of commerce for reaching out to the world at large.

It is 'widely believed that these chambers played a definite role in stalling a new "government after Deve Gowda was voted out, ensuring that the vote of account would have been passed if Gujral had not been sworn in till April 21, 1997 and to the recall of P Chidambaram in North Block as the finance minister.

Again it was for the first time that a serious bid was made during the recent political crisis to delink economy with politics and to evolve a national consensus on economic policy like its foreign counterpart. The credit for this new clout goes to the new players in the chamber arena such as India Trade Promotion Organisation (ITPO), Confederation of Indian Industries (CII) and Federation of Indian Exporters (FIEO). Old corporate war-horses including Federation of Indian Chambers Commerce and Industry (FICCI) and Associated Chambers of Commerce (ASSOCHAM) are having a tough time in redefining their roles because of the changed global scenario.

It was Chidambaram in his capacity as commerce minister in the then Rao government who gave teeth to ITPO and converted it into a most efficient and professional trade chamber.

Though each one of them claims to represent a distinctly different segment of Indian industries, but their roles seem to overlap, And that is where FICCI and ASSOCHAM are feeling beaten at their own game.

It is judged by the visiting presidents and prime ministers choosing to accept the invitations of the younger chambers. Even the ex-Prime Minister IK Gujral paid a left-handed compliment to the outgoing CII chief Shekhar Dutta when he mentioned that many a times both of them had been in the same queue seeking appointments with foreign heads and the latter being more successful than the former.

In the final analysis, they seem to be the playgrounds of captains of Indian commercial enterprises and in the process try and build a pressure group to influence the policies of the commerce and finance ministries in particular and the whole government in general. ITPO, being the only outfit in the public sector, stands out because the initiative here rests in the professional hands minus the clash of corporate egos. It is reflected in the calendar of foreign and domestic trade fairs round the year. ITPO has been instrumental in attracting a plethora of foreign participants in fairs ranging from apparels to zinc. Its permanent abode Pragati Maidan which was once condemned as a white elephant sprawlng over, banks of Yamuna today has become *sine dua non* of Indian initiative in the world trade. The same Pragati Maidan is bubbling with activities during the whole year thereby exposing Indian business to the latest global trends in manufacturing and innovations and creating an awareness about quality and competition.

Judging by the response of 100 diplomatic missions based in India it is evident that ITPO has turned out to be the proverbial tortoise amidst the sharp but complacent and monolithic corporate clubs which go by the name of chambers. Being a part of the commerce ministry, it not only represents the official mandate but is taken more seriously because of its representative character. One of the main highlights of ITPO is the two year old 40 page bi-monthly periodical *Pragati India* brought out by the information and computers division. It is an update on Indian economy, trade and industry, products, exporters fairs and exhibitions with special Focus on Latin America and Caribbean region in English as well as Spanish. This journal alone is a testimony to the professional approach of ITPO towards its function and responsibility.

Common Man and Foreign Policy

ICWA was set up soon after Independence at the initiative of Jawaharlal Nehru (who even contributed Rs 500 for building fund) to promote and propagate Indian foreign policy and our world view. The entire credit goes to Hriday Nath Kanjru and his colleagues who managed not only the council but also set up a research centre and a library which later got merged with Jawaharlal Nehru University (JNU). Now it is now known as School of International Studies (SIS). Even today, the renowned professors of JNU fondly remember their association with Sapru House and its library and its contribution in making them scholars of eminence. After SIS merger with JNU and Nehru's death ICWA fell on bad days and all activities suddenly came to a grinding halt. This continued for a decade-and-a-half. The structure and paraphernalia were all there but no one was taking any interest in its activities—*The Journal India Quarterly*. replenishment of the library, seminars, lectures, conferences, symposia and allied activities. Then came Josh and the rest is contemporary history.

There are many pressure groups like Saturday Club of the India International Centre (IIC) which reflect on international issues and provide intellectual inputs for the benefit of South Block. Now the world knows that this club has given us the present Prime Minister. But this very fact speaks about the exclusivity of these ventures. While ICWA has taken the foreign relations to the grass-roots level. I will give you an example:

One could feel the impact of the guest speaker who is representing the in-exile Rabbani government. Khalili a product of then Delhi college now known as Zakir Hussain college has perfected that the against the Taliban like a mature stage actor who spell pounds his audience the moment he inters on the stage. Khalili told the enthralled audience that the Taliban had only Kabul, but they would never be able to win Afghanistan.

He spelt out his conditions for a negotiated political settlement but apprehended that same would not be acceptable to the Taliban and their masters in Islamabad. Khalili spotted each ambassador who was present in the audience and correlated the plight of his country especially with the neighbouring Central Asian Republics (CAR). The crux of his powerful rendition was what it is not Afghanistan alone which is the target of the superpowers and their lackeys but the whole of Central Asia and its oil reserves. Many Central Asian ambassadors were nodding in total agreement. While all this drama was going on, the ordinary Indians who had no intellectual chip on their shoulders were witnessing the gory details of the civil war going on at our doorsteps across the borders. Before Khalili, Professor, Sri Prakash of Jamia and a former Indian diplomat MS Batra who had three postings in Kabul defended the Indian policy towards Afghanistan and drew identical lines between the two countries. The continuing presence of ambassador Khalili in Delhi though not being a representative of whosoever is in charge of Kabul is an example of our objective diplomatic pursuits even in the wake of adverse criticism that we should not put all the eggs in Rabbani's basket.

The moral of the evening is that it is equally important to involve the common man in foreign policy issues as the intellectuals sitting in the ivory towers. Because unless the people at large will be taken into confidence especially about our neighbours no political initiatives can succeed. The recent Indo-Pak talks are a case in point and in that sense ICWA is doing a wonderful job by taking the diplomacy to the ordinary citizen of Delhi. However, Josh would benefit ICWA and himself if he could take a little more care in handling the affairs of this prestigious organisation. The sweating ambassadors might have gone backenlightened, but the price they had to pay could hardly he called amusing.

The Way Australians Do It

As a part of my current binge on Oceania, I landed at the Australian high commission in Chanakyapuri and came back with one of the most rewarding diplomatic interactions.

Like any other mission, you are stonewalled and screened here also but once you are in, a whole new world is waiting for you. The petite but most efficient media manager Maushami Dutt wastes little time in making you feel at home and has answers to all your queries regarding Australia. She also assures that the answers she doesn't have, the battery of first secretaries and other diplomats who are experts on education, immigration, trade and culture would be too willing to give, provided they know what exactly you are looking for.

When I went through the bunch of papers I was handed over, I realised two things. In the existing scheme of things, India doesn't figure in the perspective or calculations of Melbourne. But it is very keen now to talk business with India. The 100-odd pages beautifully printed 26th edition of Australia in brief mentions Vietnam, Middle East and even Caribbean in the chapter in international relations, but India—not even once.

However, Australia-India business council has launched a colourful flier published from there which gives all relevant information on bilateral trade and its prospects including internet numbers of FICCI and even Ministry of External Affairs. The message is loud and clear.

Australian priorities are in order and well defined. Historical linkages with Great Britain (British queen is their queen and they are yet to become a republic like India), defence treaty with the US for their national security, strong ties with New Zealand and Pacific island states and enriching business contact with Japan, China, Korea and Malaysia. Their well-stocked library has a full section on Papua New Guinea. Australia is a part of Asia Pacific Economic Cooperation (APEC) and Indian Ocean Rim-Association for Regional Cooperation (IOR-ARC) and is a leading trading partner of ASEAN. We have started looking towards east rather late in the day—over 50 years after our Independence but Australia is already well-saddled in its forays in Asia. In fact, they want to give a new thrust to their western image. They held an Australian festival last year but India as an economy despite its globalised liberalisation has not impressed. A very large section of Indians have declared Australia their new favoured destination and are making a beeline to the continent but it is not for the asking. India has taken a major initiative in organising the littoral states of Indian Ocean but we don't have strong enough sinews to exert any clout. If Australia is synonymous to the continent by the same name, so is India which shares its name with a great ocean but the similarity ends there.

Nature has been rather unkind to Australia. A large portion of its northern territory is inhospitable but the progress made in the rest has more than compensated. Like India, Australia also has a significant population of indigenous people but its commission for indigenous and Torres Strait islander people could be a good lesson to our commission of the scheduled castes and scheduled tribe. Australia doesn't have a glorious past of more than 5,000 years like India. It was discovered only a few centuries ago by European travellers but their dedication and devotion has made them into a bubbling cosmopolitan country with 140 nationalities in absolute harmony. It is strange but true that Indian understanding of the Australians is still confined to the cricketing fields where our teams meet at regular intervals and the occasional advertisements by Australians promising Indian students greener pastures in education and career. But it is time when we wake up to each other's potential and take some bold steps.

Academic Tribute to Narayanan

There are well laid down traditions of *guru-shishya parampara* and *guru-dakshina* in Indian academic ethos. But like so many other traditions these have also been commercialised.

Therefore, when I spotted a book – *State and Society in Latin America,* challenges of globalisation edited by Abdul Nafey, Vishnu Priya and Dalbir Singh, it came to me as a pleasant surprise. The book consists of specially written articles by Satya R Pattnayak, Chintamani Mahapatra, R L Chawla, Rodolfo Bermejo, Priti Singh, Father George Madeikkal, Seema Ashok Raj, Ritu Jain, Tushar Kant and Ravindranathan P, and the three editors.

Barring the Mexican journalist Rodolfo who is reporting India to local media back home, all have been students of a distinguished scholar on Latin America— R Narayanan who recently retired from Jawahar Lal

Nehru university after teaching for more than three decades.

These students, some of whom are now professors in their own right, have dedicated the writings in the book to their guru Narayanan. I have not seen a better example of *guru-shishya parampara* and this form of *guru dakshina.*

Narayanan's dedication and commitment to Latin American studies is manifest in the 13 PhDs and more than a score of MPhils, he has produced during his stint at the JNU

There are few parallels in the academic world of such single mindedness. Narayanan is an Indian Latin Americanist of International reckoning and if instead of guiding his students, he had spent this time on his own pursuit, he might have been looming large on the international Latin American horizon in an Oxford, Cambridge, Stanford or a Yale. But he chose to understand and explain the eldorado-turned enigma lying between the Gulf of Mexico and Tierradel Fuego.

Narayanan has consciously chosen to nurture his students in place of self-aggrandisement. He has avoided putting his thoughts between the covers of books but his students will vouch that their PhD and MPhil dissertations are the expansions of his analyses and interpretations.

If he had emulated his peers and contemporaries, he would have been an author of as many books, as the number of thesis, he has opted to supervise. But he in his wisdom thought that the practitioners of Latin American studies would be a better bet rather than unread books shelved in the libraries and the personal collection of the friends and admirers. Who knows, today, when he sits back at his desk he might be amused at the glory his students have covered themselves with, in different parts of the world.

However, the history of Latin American studies in India is full of non-events. The student join this programme with a lot of enthusiasm but when they pass out after years of toil and sweating, they realise there are no takes of their knowledge. Some of the more enterprising ones move over to greener pasteures in the west but most of them end up as generalists despite being specialists.

Latin America doesn't fall under the priority areas of UGC's consideration. When the time came to set up the first area studies centre in this country, instead of choosing the JNU which had become the sole repository of the academic excellence in this field, it opted for Goa because once upon a time that was a Portuguese colony and therefore a natural link with Latin America. The mandarins in the UGC would not know that the former Portuguese colony Brazil fights shy in calling itself a Latin American country.

The high-handed decision of the UGC resulted in a non-performing area studies centre at Goa as compared to the highly productive programme at the JNU, earlier stops churning out scholars in Latin America, Goa centre might neither find the teachers nor the researchers.

Since Latin America is not taught as a subject in any other university apart from the JNU and Goa, there are no avenues for the scholars in the subject. Those who still opt to join colleges, end up teaching the subjects they studied at the MA.

The bilateral and multilateral trade, with that region refuses to cross the one per cent rubicon, therefore the chambers and private sector have nothing to offer to the Latin Americanists.

Despite being a block of 46 countries including 33 votes at the UN and other multinational fora, and a significant 15 lac population of Indian origin craving for their roots, Latin America is not the favourite concerns of the foreign policy formulations.

At least, the ministry of external affairs has an independent desk for the region but the commerce ministry like Bill Clinton, still considers it as the backyard of the US.

Therefore, the erudite tributes of Narayana's students ranging from democratisation to globalisation through liberalisation in different Latin American countries are painstaking studies of a grateful generation of the pupils but apparently destined to be scholastic than pragmatic.

Gifts from Venezuela

The Venezuelan ambassador Walter Marquez has sent me three books published by him. The chosen subjects reveal which way his mind is working. One of them contains three profiles of the Latin American liberator Simon Bolivar, the second is the Spanish translation of Bhagwat Gita and the third is his lecture delivered in Cairo to the members of COTAL—the association of the travel agents from that region.

In his lecture he has emphasised on the need to relax and liberalise the rules governing passports and visas. It is apparent that the ambassador is aiming at bringing people closer by cutting red tape and by understanding each other's culture and ethos.

The profiles of Bolivar have a universal appeal. For example, he had prescribed capital punishment to those who misuse or appropriate even ten pesos and that should apply to judges as well. Bolivar wanted to unite Latin America as a single political entity. And he was always suspicious of the American designs. He did succeed for a while but that was shortlived. Little did he know that one day a similar initiative would come from the big brother to form an all American free trade area on the lines of NAFTA. If Bolivar is the mascot of a hypothetical united Latin America, Bhagwat Gita is the ultimate insignia of Indian ethos which doesn't preach any religion but as a way of life based on the theory of action.

Gita has been rendered in almost every important language of the world including Spanish but this particular translation by Mora Singh has kept in mind her ultimate reader. That is why she has used just one name each for Krishna and Arjuna so that the hispanic reader is not confused. Similarly, she has simplified the theory of karma, yoga and devotion.

One may not count these efforts in the traditional mould of diplomacy. Such publications are not spelt out in MoUs and joint commissions but these are born out of the visions of the likes of Walter Marquez.

Dixit's Diplomatic Diaries

We all know that the former foreign secretary JN Dixit is a gacious reader, prolific writer and articulate commentator on diplomacy, but he is also a meticulous diarist who maintained graphic details of the day to day events of his long and distinguished career in foreign service aming to light only now.

He is already four books old, understandably he has covered Pakistan, Sri Lanka and now Afghanistan in three of his four books was India's envoy in each of countries. There is another common factor in these three books. One of them have been published by mark for which the energetic and freighted publisher KPR Nair serves all kudos from the serious fraternity. In present times in publishers are busy making a buck through quickies such an artist highly laudable. Dixit's latest book an Afghan diary: Sir Shah to Taliban was released by ICR security advisor RN Rao at a ministerial function at India International Centre, unlike the usual release ceremonies this one was marked by the erudite presentations from former ambassador and presently the vice-chancellor of Aligarh Muslim university, MH Ansari and the most wanted strategic analyst C Raja Mohan of the Hindu. All the Speakers raised pertinent questions about India's Afghan policy which lost its track in 1980s and never got it on to desirable course.

Link with Mexico Launched

With the return of Pedro Gonzalez-Rubio S again as the ambassador of Mexico a lot of good news is arriving. Week's post brought 36-page magazine link with Mexico published by its ministry of external affairs. Perhaps the first magazine of its kind which only talks about the publisher country but the whole region from political, diplomatic, economic and cultural perspective the last piece is penned by none else than Octavio Paz who instantly fell in love with India as well found his lady love here during his extended six-year tenure as ambassador of India in 1960s.

Artistically designed and impeccably edited journal will serve both as an interesting reading as well as useful reference reckoner. Along with this came an invitation 10 six medical feature films to be screened at India International Centre.

RC Shukla has seen half of the world as an Indian ambassador. But today he has chosen to fill not only world with the bright colours spread by his wife Kusum but also of those beholders who are left awe-truck at the first exposure. It was a pleasant surprise to see Shukla manning the Lalit Kala Akademi art gallery at Rabindra Bhawan, where umpteenth solo exhibition by Kusum Shukla was on display.

Generally the Indian male, because of his chauvinism, is not known to put his ego in the shadows of his wife but the manner in which Shukla took pains to explain each and every etching and the shade of colours of his wife's painting unveiled a proud husband and a noble man beneath and stiff upper-lipped diplomat: Kusum's paintings adorn in private collections in Europe, Africa and Latin America.

Remembering his days, in Trinidad and Tobago he recalled the important position Indian High Commissioners enjoy in that twin-island nation on the fringe of the South American continent bordering the Atlantic. Contrary to popular perception Shukla feels India should not interfere in the internal affairs of other countries even if the Indians are in formidable numbers. Though he was posted in port of Spain in early 1980s but his unorthodox views are quite relevant even today.

Global Diplomacy

The other day while entering the building of YMCA in Jai Singh road in Delhi I overheard a conversation between the two students seeking admission in one of the professional courses offered by the association regarding what was the full form of YMCA. None knew. This bit speaks volumes about the self-effacing but humanitarian activities of a Christian organisation (hope anti-Christian activists are listening).

YMCA and its sister association YWCA are the only global outfits which are engaged in the holistic upliftment of the youth of the world. Though founded on the catholic principles of Christianity they are not known for spreading the gospels of the Christ.

YMCA's untiring efforts uniting the global youth is the best example of the universality of the mankind enshrined in the preachings of the Christ. No wonder YMCA is gaining in stature and popularity as reflected from the second branch of its professional institute in Nizamuddin.

Where Book is a World

Disinvestment in public sector is in the air. Still there are some government enterprises which need to be protected like the species under the danger of being extinct. One of such organisations is National book trust (NBT) which is known for inexpensive books containing invaluable treasure of knowledge.

Though the primary function of the NBT is to bring the different regions closer by publishing the Indian writers in all languages but it also undertakes to bring home the world literature. According to its Director Nirmal Kanti Bhattacharjee it has already published Stories from Vietnam, Israel and the Asia Pacific region. The anthologies from Korea are on the anvil.

The publication of the world literature in Indian languages is a noble but an unfashionable task which no private sector publisher would like to venture. In a free economy driven by market forces such efforts are generally swept away with the winds of change but world of books should be preserved at all costs because this is the oldest tool to achieve globalisation.

Education Industry of Australia

My formative years were based on the myth that you needed brilliance or billions to study abroad. What to talk of getting admission, getting to know which university offered what was shrouded in mystery but these days every morning begins with newspaper advertisements hawking admission to an Australian university for the asking. I used to wonder how come Australian education was available abegging until when I was invited to a higher education bazaar at the Durbar hall of Taj Palace. Universities such as the Melbourne, Bond, Queensland and Monash had put up stalls to sell their courses for Indian students. Elegantly dressed

Australians were manning the counters to answer all sorts of queries from higher education seekers. The bazaar called Australian education expo was declared open by JNU vice-chancellor Ashish Dutta. Australian high commissioner Darren P Gribble along with his education and training counsellor Tom Calma were there to lend the whole exercise an official stamp. I was told that education was one of the biggest foreign exchange earning export-oriented industry in Australia and such bazaars were held in most of the south east and south Asian countries to attract foreign students to their country.

According to Australian international education foundation, the country was already earning more than Australian $ 2 billion [1 Aus $ = Rs 28 (1995)] every year by way of export earnings and it was projected to go up to four billion by the turn of millennium. The foundation launched a journal called *Education Dialogue* on the occasion highlighting the education opportunities in that country. According to this journal, Australia was spending five per cent of its gross domestic product (GDP) as against 3.55 spent by India on high education. In 1995 there were 52,000 (8.6 per cent of the total students) foreign students studying for their tertiary degrees including more than 4,000 from India alone. There are more than 50 universities and their affiliated colleges to choose from. Being an English-speaking Commonwealth country like India and also a multicultural society, Indian students fit perfectly—both in the classroom and outside. According to counsellor Calma Indian students are high achievers.

All this might indicate that Australia is distributing tertiary degrees by charging exhorbitant fees from the rich and affluent sections of the Indian society. But that is not a fact. There are dropouts and black sheep who try to use this opportunity to find employment. And an admission doesn't automatically entitle the applicant for a visa. According to the education manager and editor of *Education Dialogue,* all normals for visa and foreign exchange apply as in case of every other foreigner seeking entry to Australia.

Australia is a unique case which has converted its academic reservoir into an industry without compromising with its quality and standard. Today, one doesn't necessarily require an Anglo-Saxon degree in a job market. Australia is a giving a tough time to the traditional degrees from Western hemisphere and at one-third of price. One needs US $ 22,000 for an American degree every year while in Australia it is available for Australian $ 7500.

In the question-answer-sessions conducted at the bazaar, Indian students were rightly curious to know why such degrees are not available in India. They were told that the education was similar but the application not. Meaning, the learning was not related to market needs. One could not change courses and colleges mid-stream without losing grades in the process. In fact education is so cheap because of the state subsidy in India that it was more of a past-time till you knock the job market that nobody really bothered about.

Not that India doesn't offer courses for foreign students and also there is no dearth of academicians and experts in higher education but no one has thought to convert it into an industry. We are offering numerous scholarships to Asian and African students to create goodwill. All that is fine but if Indian students can create wonders after studying here, why Indian universities can't make their degrees market-friendly.

The professional competence of our doctors, engineers and software developers is globally recognised. If Indian professionals are accepted the world over—including Australia—why can't we attract foreign students on internationally competitive market rates? Why can't we also declare our higher education an industry and let the foreign students pay for themselves as well as ours?

Diary of an Endless Yugoslav Night

It was a diplomatic party with a difference. There were ambassadors, other diplomats, writers, professors, publishers, journalists and of course socialites. Yet it did not have the stiffness or the formal veneer of a National Day celebration. It was the occasion of release of the book by Khushwant Singh of *Night and Day–A Diary,* a book written by Dr. Mira Markovic, wife of the President of Yugoslavia and a professor at the University of Belgrade.

The release was held at the Maurya to a packed audience that listened intently to the remarks of Khushwant Singh, the author Mira Markovic and Prof SK Jha of Jawaharlal Nehru University, who promptly invited the writer to address his East European division students at the JNU.

Wives of political leaders are known for social causes and charity campaigns but this book is a painful political study of a strife-torn nation.

The reasons are not difficult to understand. It is a reminder of the trade happenings between 1992-93.

The book as well as the lady are products of a situation which has changed the course of contemporary history.

When destiny places you in a vantage position on the centre stage of your nation, either you become a rebel or a philosopher.

I must in all honesty mention here that the informal atmosphere of the occasion, despite the sober and thought–provoking subject of the book was the effort of the organisers–the East West publishers and the public relations outfit of Dilip Cherian. Perfect Relations themselves.

The scotch poured like mineral water and long stemmed crystal glasses glimmered in the light full to the brim with red wine, trying to drown the painful thoughts generated by the preceding release function–a bitter commentary on the sad times we live in.

The event is also a living witness to the continued good relations that India and Yugoslavia share though trade has received a setback. It also manifests an interaction at a popular level between the intellectuals of the two countries notwithstanding the official positions.

India was one of the major contributors to the UN peace-keeping force under the command of General Satish Nambiar to the separated Yugoslav republic of Bosnia-Herzegovina.

Certain powers in the now unipolar world successfully tried to dismember the erstwhile Yugoslavia but failed to disfigure the name of Yugoslavia from the world map.

India was one of the rare countries who relentlessly supported, the Yugoslav identity even while accepting the cruel reality of separated new nations like Bosnia, Croatia and Macedonia.

It is heartening to note that many more countries of the world are re-recognising the existence of Yugoslavia as a sovereign nation of Serbs despite having contributed to the civil war in the newly constituted South Slav nations.

The neighbouring West European nations are facing the guilt oven the fact that most of the bullets shot in Europe in recent history were in the Balkans.

According to Mira Markovie, south Slav nations and all the people living in the Balkans have no choice but to live together if they hope to survive in historical terms.

As a columnist it is a moral dilemma for me whether to empathise with Mira for the suffering she and her nation have faced or to be envious of her magical words and lyrical style through which she has given meaning to her own life, not only at a personal level but for the benefit of her people and times.

Wanted an African Cultural Centre

During my two successive visits to African continents in 1995 to Burkina Faso and Ghana and Zimbabwe and Namibia in Southern Africa with the then Prime Minister PV Narasimha Rao and President Shankar Dayal Sharma, I found that the great adaptability of African singers even to the Indian melodies of 1940s and 50s.

I vividly remember the moist eyes of Indian and African leaders when an African singer, after a couple of his local numbers, suddenly burst the atmosphere with a high voltage Indian film song. That evening was a pointer towards the potential of Indo-African cultural interaction and integration.

I am sure an African cultural centre will become the nerve centre such a confluence of two cultures divergent in form, but convergent in content. Sudan, the largest African country, is generally in news for reasons other than diplomacy. There are more than three thousand Sudanese students in India—one of the largest contingents of unofficial ambassador from its country. About hundred study in various institutions in Delhi. A dozen of them being on scholarship under bilateral cultural exchange programme. They enjoy total freedom of expression to the extent of raising the voice of dissidence against their own political dispensation. Sudanese embassy is pretty cool about these activities despite its regimented image perpetuated by the Western media which continues to portray it in all dark shades.

Said Abdel Rehman Sharfi, 'first secretary in the embassy there, "our students have been getting Indian visa on a platter from Indian embassy in Khartoum because of the liberal policies pursued by India towards all African nations. Not all African students engaged themselves seriously in their academic persuits in India. Some get politicised. Others overstay and some even indulge in unawful activities. But India has never allowed this to become a bone of contention with the concerned country. Of late, there have been evidences of some Europe-based human rights organisations funding and patronising student organisations from such third world countries whose political preferences do not fall in line with the western model. Sudan is one of them. Sudanese students are divided in as many groups as exist in the country back home and there have been cases of fierce arguments and at times minor violence after heated altercations. A small restaurant in the bylanes of the crowded Nizamudin is a case in point. Rival groups use its walls for their ongoing debate on political differences. Sudanese students throng to this restaurant for the latest arguments about the internal situation of the country.

Some students even use the columns of Indian media to air their grievances against their own government. Some even seek political asylum and consequent financial help from United Nations Commissions on human right.

But Sudanese government has neither sought the deportation of any student nor tried to impound their passport. Its policy is to allow any lawful political activity even on a foreign soil because it believes in the basic human rights and dignity.

Sudan has more than 200 languages and 300 tribes which account for some of the ethnic tension in the country. Its people stand out among African community by its distinct colour which they prefer to call as no colour.

The official language is Arabic but most of them understand and use English. Sudan is one of those rare countries which supported India in its abortive bid to a non-permanent seat in Security Council and doesn't mince words in accepting it. It supports India on the issue of Kashmir even in a predominant anti-India Organisation of Islamic countries. India needs to reciprocate African overtures like the forthcoming Sudanese cultural centre by reciprocating cultural exchanges and intensifying the exposure of Africa through ICCR which at times seems to be Eurocentric like our economic and political diplomacy. Some 3000-odd students from Sudan and its many more multiples from other African countries could well be used as a repository of Indian-hospitality turned into interactive diplomacy.

Move over IIC, Here Comes IHC

At last the wait is over! Much to the delight of the 53,500-odd members who had been waiting for almost five years, the India Habitat Centre (IHC) opened its gates and laid out an impressive array of foodstalls around the lush green lawns. The much awaited centre also announced a series of cultural and intellectual programmes in the days to come before it formally starts half a dozen restaurants and bars to meet the varied tastes of the elite and the professionals of the Capital. A trailer of its intentions was manifest in the two Hindi plays *Rishte-naate* and *Tunhari Amrita* staged in the artistically designed auditoria. Even the Sunday morning was filled with classical ragas of celebrated vocalist Dagar.

Though India Habitat Centre had let out its office space to many national and international organisations a couple of years ago, the hospitality sector ran into trouble over some trivial issues which was thankfully settled thus ending the agony of its members. Finally, it has remained in the hands of the Old World Hospitality of the hotel Broadway and restaurant Chor Bizzare fame. The taste bud of diplomatic circles in Delhi are not unfamiliar with the Old World charm, as the latter has been regularly organising parties in Delhi and other such cities as Hyderabad.

It is not a pure coincidence that IHC is located at a proverbial stones throw distance from the Old citadel of intellectual and diplomacy called the India International Centre (IIC). There are many stories doing the rounds of the Capital as to why and how IHC came about. One of the most popular being the denial of IIC membership to some high and mighty in the bureaucracy who successfully vowed to build a far superior centre exactly *tere ghar ke samne*. But that is where my fear rests.

And I hope that IHC does not get rapped in the same mould. A cursory glance at the constitution of IIC tells you about its lofty ideals the basic thrust was to create a nuclear of activity to expose its members to the contemporary international issues through dialogue, lectures, films and other plastic and performing arts. Notwithstanding that IIC has given the country its first diplomatic Prime Minister along with a principal secretary, N Vohra, who was serving as its director before moving to the sylvan surroundings of the Raisina Hills. But that cannot condone its straying into bizzare directions which was never stipulated at the time of its inception. Today the most important venues at IIC are its dining hall, coffee lounge and the bar. Not even its library which is considered to be one of the best in Delhi. Barring a singular exception of the former governor of Jammu and Kashmir Jagmohan who has produced many fabulous books with its help, no one seems to be using it more seriously than a newspaper reading room. Its much touted Saturday club and diplomatic, political and economic fora are dominated by a handful of retired foreign secretaries and a chosen few editors who have formed a mutual appreciation club to scratch each other's back. The nationally renowned Saturday club behaves like a coterie of intellectuals shutting the doors to any new enthusiasts. Its publications are irregular and indifferent, its journal has nothing to do with international relations and its guest house has become the den for politicians including ND Tiwari and Devendra Diwedi who despite having their houses in Delhi use it to hold political conclaves.

The profile of IIC membership betrays the trust of its initiators. The majority of IIC consists of the bureaucrats and the businessmen who have nothing to do either with international relations or the fine arts. It is evident from the miniscule attendance at the cultural functions, discussions and lectures, it was shocked to see the half empty auditorium when the Brazilian president Cardoso came to address its members. Unfortunately the monthly information pamphlet does not give any tempting information about the forthcoming programmes to prompt the members to come. It is presumed that the members are initiated in every activity of the centre. Their absence shows that they are not.

Now coming back to the Habitat Centre which has also been established with similar high sounding aspirations to provide a platform for synergical development of man and his surroundings. IHC has begun on a very promising note as far as its architecture is concerned which according to the environment professor Sharma of Jawaharlal Nehru University (JNU) is one of the best three eco-friendly buildings in Delhi—the other two being the immunology centre near JNU and the Belgian ambassador's residence which was designed by Satish Gujral and declared as one of the best 100 buildings of the century. But IHC will have to be very careful in charting out its agenda. It should not give in to the popular demands of its members the way the IIC has done. It should also refrain from being a clone of the IIC.

If America's former secretary of state James Baker succeeds in his initiatives to hold the long overdue referendum for the right of self-determination of Sahrawis in the Sahara desert, he would be paying a befitting tribute to San Houston who liberated Texas from the Mexicans in 1836.

In the city of Houston, named after San Houston, Baker clinched the much awaited settlement between the Sahrawis and the Moroccans in the presence of the Algerians and the Mauritanians.

Houston should not be unfamiliar to Indians as it is the city where the rich and the politicians of this country have been rushing to for by-pass surgery.

It is also the same economically vibrant city where then Prime Minister Narasima Rao opened the fourth consulate of India a couple of years ago after Chicago, New York and San Francisco.

Baker has shown what a successful diplomat can achieve even after hanging his gloves. He has set up a conflict resolving institute in the south of US and has kept two of the world's outstanding crisis situations on his agenda—Western Sahara and Cyprus.

He claimed last fortnight after brokering a deal between Moroccans and Sahrawis that 80,000-odd legitimate inhabitants of western Sahara would be able to decide whether they want an independent nation or want to live under Moroccan rule.

Sahara is the last outpost of the Europeans colonisation of Africa which for last 20 years has been suffering on account of the mechanisations of the former rulers. Spain gave them independence but by strange sequence of events—two-thirds and one-thirds of their land was taken over by the neighbouring Morocco and Mauritania respectively.

The latter withdrew in 1979, paving way for their liberation under the leadership of Polisario (Polar front for the liberation of Saguia, Al Hamr a and Riod Oro).

Morocco disputes this and claims that historically the whole land belonged to them. In this bloody conflict, families got divided amongst the territory occupied by Morocco—under the control of Polisario—and the refugee camps in Algeria.

When Spaniards left in 1976, the population of the 40 Sahrawis tribes was around 76,000. That is why Baker has estimated that the survivors among this population and their genuine descendants would be counted for the purpose of referendum. That is where the challenge lies. Apart from these genuine and original habitants of Sahara, there are an estimated two lakh people each, both in the Algerian camps and the territory under Moroccan control.

One doesn't know-how many of the Sahrawis have crossed over to Morocco or Algeria. Needless to say that Morocco claims people on all the three sides are genuine Sahrawis and should be counted while giving the choice for referendum.

That has been the position of Rabat for the last 20 years and that is why despite so many UN interventions, Sahrawis have not agreed to it. They are convinced that the people living on the Moroccan side are the officers and men in uniform (Moroccan police and army) or the fifth columnists who have pushed in the name of Sahrawis. Now that's a ticklish issue.

Baker's intention could be noble but the head count would be difficult. Much will depend on the superpowers who are going to sit this month, in the Security Council, to adopt the deal served by Baker after a series of prolonged discussions shuttled between Lisbon and London and finally landing in Housing.

Sahrawis believe that the US has been able to prevail upon King Hasa of Morocco who has been heading a constitutional monarchy in northwest Africa since 1961 by showing him the threat of the rising Islamic fundamentalism which is causing a great unrest in the neighbouring Algeria. Though he has been a moderate king in the modern democratic times, the evil designers of religious strife spares no model of democracy and secularism.

Then there is another problem. Suppose Sahrawis win the vote and their land from Moroccans, what will they do with almost two lakh people which they would be offered on a platter by Morocco alongwith the land? The same United Nations which is trying to barter a deal for them would come in the shape of a human rights commission for a humanitarian approach towards the plethora of people whom Sahrawis today dismiss as planted Moroccans. Even if they are could they be uprooted from their adopted land and wished away into Mediterranean?

However, these are post-referendum issues. Much before this happens, many other hurdles would have to be crossed. As far as India is concerned, it has always been sympathetic towards the Sahrawis cause. The present political dispensation comprising of IK Gujral, Inderjit Gupta and Harkishan Singh Surjeet have always supported Sahara's freedom and its opening an embassy here.

But somewhere in between, partly because of Moroccan pressure and mainly because of the position taken by the Organisation of African Unity (OAU) that only a fair and free referendum can decide the real status of Sahrawis people and land. India played indifferent to the requests for a new Sahara ambassador in New Delhi. The latest developments must have sent right signals.

Reaching out to the World

There are many governmental and non-governmental organisations which take silent but broad diplomatic initiatives in order to reach out to the world. One of such outfits is United Service Institute of India (USI) headed by the retired decorated General Nambiar.

This institute is devoted to the task of providing platforms to the internationally renowned diplomats and learned scholars for the benefit of Indian experts in uniform and otherwise. Earlier it used to be in the prohibitive confines of Kashmir House on Rajaji Marg. Now it has moved into its own building in the friendly environs of the defence complexes on way to the international airport.

I attended a lecture by the articulate and convincing Egyptian ambassador in India, Cillani Allam on the peace prospects in West Asia. Former foreign secretary JN Dixit, who presided over the proceedings, informed the audience that the learned and experienced ambassador was a post-graduate from Princeton University, had played a significant role in the National Commission set up to assess the compensation due from Iraq and had represented her country in Yugoslavia, UN, and Austria before being appointed as ambassador to India. The audience comprised of retired and serving Indian generals and diplomats from many countries, including China and Iran, as well as top governmental functionaries.

In next one hour, the distinguished speaker shared her concerned and vision about West Asia in an impassioned but restrained eloquence.

According to her, America has always been a natural broker in Middle East and it will always stand to gain whichever side wins. But it has lost any moral authority it had over Israel who today considers herself as the only superpower left in the unipolar world. Today, even if

Washington wants to apply any brakes on Tel Aviv, it will have no effect on Netanyahu.

Ambassador Allam had not brought any written speech. But with the help of some scribbled notes, she kept the audience enthralled and spell-bound. The crux of her discourse was that Israel was behaving in an irrational and unjustified manner by violating all norms, conventions and even agreements and understanding in the occupied territories on the East and West Banks of the river Jordan.

Inexplicably, it doesn't want to discuss even any of the contentious issues at the UN and is deliberately creating conditions lending to conflict and confrontation.

Narrating the historical course of the crisis, she remembered the almost suicidal peace visit of her late president Anwar Sadat in November 1977 where he had offered peace and no war. But Israel in turn fell short of reciprocating. Prime Minister Benin had said he would take peace, no war offer but would not give up Jerusalam.

Later while answering questions the lady ambassador accepted a unilateral suggestion as an Egyptian that she was a game to convert Jerusalem into an international holy city like the Vatican. Incidentally, now it is being revealed that the same idea was acceptable to general Moshe Dayan of Israel, but with the condition that the city would be governed by Israel.

Ambassador paid a left handed compliment to BBC and CNN for putting fire at the ashes of peace process in Middle East. She ridiculed the western model of global village if it was based on sowing the seeds of discord in the name of bridging the geographical distances. But she was still hopeful that the fate of nations and humans could still be decided by conversation instead of confrontation.

According to her perception, Israel was creating new enemies in West Asia, namely Iran and Islam. They have neutralised Egypt and Jordan, taken care of Iraq and now are engrossed in humiliating and belittling Palestinians. She wanted a firm commitment for law and peace from Israel, withdrawal from all occupied territories forcibly occupied in 1967, acceptance of Palestinian statehood and right of self-determination talks with Syria and Lebanon.

She said Netanyahu could reconcile to his dreams but let him be fair and dignified. She ended on a note of ironical acceptance of Huddington's theory of clash of civilisations in the next century between Islam and Christianity. She didn't agree with the theory but conceded that the world seemed to heading towards that.

Not many ambassadors speak with such candour and honesty. USI deserves praises for exposing the Indian enquiring minds to such international insights by providing platforms to such indulgent speakers.

Dharmshila to Panchsheel as Rescue

The Diplomatic Enclave of Chanakyapuri was conceived on the basic tenets of peaceful co-existence among nations. They were pronounced by the great ancient statesman of India, Chanakya, also known as Kaulilya, in the court of Chandragupta. These tenets known as *dharma* (conduct), *niti* (diplomacy), *satya* (truth), *nyaya* (justice), and *shanti* (peace). That is why various roads, lanes and even bylanes have been named after these principles and their original propaganist. These five tenets are based on mutual faith and trust which are rare commodities these days because of bias, prejudice and discrimination of all hues and shades.

One of such pre-conceived notions in the diplomatic community is that medial facilities in the capital are virtually non-existent. There is a general impression that diplomats take the first flight back home or to Singapore or Hong Kong whenever, God forbid, they are indisposed. That might have been the case of a decade ago but not any more.

Hospitals like Holy Angels (Vasant Vihar), G M Modi and Chikitsa (Saket) and Veerawali (Chanakyapuri) and the latest addition, Dharmshila Cancer Hospital (Noida) can take care of any emergency or chronic ailment, matching international standards anywhere in the world. Dharmshila Cancer Hospital set up by Dr Suversha Khanna in the memory of her late father who became a sudden victim of this dreadful disease, is one of best examples of what Indian expertise in medical care as well as infrastructure building can do. Dharmshila, in Indian ethos, means the way of life consciously adopted by the protagonist to interact with fellow beings. It's a great thought to name a hospital based on such a noble philosophy.

Frankly speaking, India has suffered from the third world syndrome in medical facilities to the effect that British high commission had to set up a medical centre on its premises to provide first aid not only to its own diplomats but to its counterparts in New Delhi. However if a diplomat needed medical attention beyond the routine indisposition he preferred to rush out of this country rather than to hazard a risk.

But over a period of time Indian doctors have been able to convince the diplomats that even in leading hospitals abroad, more often than not, it is the Indian doctors who have earned a name for themselves. "It is not the doctors but the general unhygienic conditions prevalent in Delhi hospitals which put them off," opined a cross-section of diplomats contacted by this columnist. But more and more hospitals are taking utmost care on this score. It is no wonder then that the stacks of embassy files, pertaining to diplomat patients in hospitals like Holy Angels are mounting every year.

Recently, when Delhi suffered an onslaught of the mysterious dengue fever, Dharmshila Cancer Hospital provided the life saving blood placelets to the entire city hospitals because of their ultra modern technology to separate the vital blood cells. The hospital also did not charge the proverbial pound of flesh. This hospital justifiably boasts of a dust and bacteria free environment because of Laminar flow air-conditioning system, non-existent in any other hospital.

Not only diplomats but also Indians from a cross-section of the population have been making a beeline to the likes of Slone Kettring Heart Institutes of Houston "But today," claims Dr Khanna, "no one, Indian or foreigner, need to cross the outskirts of Delhi for ruling out the possibility of a cancerous growth or a definite treatment of early detection."

Such claims are supported by the ambassadors of Senegal, Kenya and many other African countries whose large student population have been receiving adequate operational and post-operational nursing at the hands of Dr Rikhi and his staff at Holy Angels.

Diplomacy is not practiced by ambassadors and their colleagues from the air-conditioned confines of the palatial chanceries. Every citizen of this country, wherever he is, can make or mar the country's image through his hospitality and fair play.

Hospitals are the ideal place for exhibiting diplomacy and hospitality because a human being is most vulnerable when in physical discomfort.

And if the host country can't take care of its guests (in this field), it has no business carrying out the lofty tenets of Chanakya. Naming roads after ideals is a good gesture but we also need substance to support the high flying ideals.

8
Diplomatic Space

Musical Chairs in the 'Embassy Bazaar'

When I contacted the Khyrgystan embassy at their A block premises in Vasant Vihar, I was told it had shifted to the adjoining B block. The same premises had been rented out to an airline representative of the Kazakhstan airlines. I was surprised to hear that, as it was only recently that the Khyrgz had moved there.

On enquiring I was told that a kind of a musical chair game was being played between the embassies and landlords in Delhi.

The south Delhi landlords have found an easy prey in the foreign missions because of the law being in their favour.

Since the contract is between the landlord and the chancery and not any individual, it has to be automatically vacated after the expiry of the deed.

It is no wonder then that Tejinder Singh of Skipper infamy was able to be rent out his palatial building on Aurangzeb road to Israelis.

This despite being in a soup on account of his shady deals with other customers.

Today, the building is about to be auctioned with Israelis tucked in safely as any legal action on the building would have no bearing on the tenant as per the contract.

Talking about tenants, an interesting situation arose in the case of the erstwhile East German embassy on Nyayamarg when the Berlin wall fell and the country got merged with its western half-brother.

The new "tenant" asked the landlady Vijayaraje Scindia to hand over possession as they were the inheritors of all rights and properties of the erstwhile East Germany. But Rajmata showed them the Indian law book which said after the "demise" of the tenant the property automatically reverts back to the landlord.

This interesting case involving diplomacy, politics and law as well as real estate was finally clinched in favour of the Germans though after some frantic behind-the - scene activities.

On the same note, our first prime minister Jawaharlal Nehru, the then magnanimous statesman that he was, had offered that the entire diplomatic enclave be named after the great Indian strategist and theoretician Chanakya, popularly known as Chanakyapuri.

It was almost like an El Dorado for the countries who accepted the offer on a reciprocal basis which some cynics describe as the great landgrab of the 1950s. Some did not make the mission as late as the 90s, the latest being Sudan and Qatar who are building it now. Interestingly enough, Sudan got it's share from the land originally alloted to Yugoslavia.

The fateful disintegration of Soviet Union changed the diplomatic map of New Delhi in which Kazakhstan got half of the Bulgarian chancery to set up its mission. Other former Soviet republics sought the help of the erstwhile big brother, either for an embassy or to house their diplomats.

It is strange but true that the Soviet Union has managed to get the maximum number of properties, scattered all over Delhi from Vasant Vihar to Barakhamba to Bhagwan Das Road.

Smaller countries like Chile, Panama, Cuba, Vietnam and Cambodia, however have to change their addresses almost every couple of years because of the "fleecing tendencies' in the real estate market. Many diplomats are on record saying that Delhi is the costliest capital for embassies in the world, next only to Tokyo.

Some are even seriously thinking of closing down their missions and operate from another capital with frequent visits to New Delhi.

Hence also the reason why many countries dread to come here and prefer concurrent accreditions like Burkina Faso operating from Beijing and Costa Rica from Tokyo.

South Block is concerted over the situation. It has offered a large piece of land in Vasant Vihar to those countries who are shuttling between Vasant Vihar and Golf Links, South Extension and Defence Colony, East of Kailash and Chirag Enclave.

In many such cases the ambassadors residences is far more majestic and spacious than their chancery. Chile, Venezuela, Mexico and Colombia fall in that category.

All this has resulted in a mushrooming of the real estate business among those specialising in diplomatic premises. It is a bazaar like situation where the landlord of Cuban ambassador ask her to vacate but in the next breath give it to Portugal on the Chileans requested to vacate on the pretext of landlords personal reasons and then renting it to the Turkmens.

Countries like America, France and Britain who are well saddled in their sprawling well stacked missions on both sides of Shantipath cannot appreciate the predicament of the smaller countries from Asia, Africa and Latin America.

These countries divide their attention between finding a new house for their missions and themselves before the expiry of their annual contract and the challenging task of putting bilateral diplomacy on an even keel in the fast growing global scenario.

Germans and Scindias Vie Over Chancery Building

The Chancery building of the erstwhile East German embassy at 2, Nyaya Marg, in New Delhi continues to be a bone of contention between the unified German embassy and its landlady, Vijaya Raje Scindia, even after six months of German unification.

In most of the countries the assets and liabilities have been settled once for all, but because of peculiar tenancy laws in India, this prized piece of property seems to be heading towards a diplomatic, political and financial imbroglio.

Though Germans refused to make any official comment about the goings-on, a senior diplomat handling press relations told *The Independent* that the external affairs ministry of India had permitted the chancery to shift the German school from another posh locality of the capital—Friends Colony—to this disputed building.

The landlord of the school building had requested the shifting of the school elsewhere. However, the urban development ministry is sitting pretty over the file, while a functionary of the Scindia empire said, "Under no circumstances would that be allowed." The then East Germans had taken this beautiful building from Vijaya Raje Scindia in 1970 for a monthly rent of Rs 3,000. Since then the rent has been revised many times. The present rate is Rs 40,000 per month and it has been paid in advance upto June 1991.

The Scindias don't want to extend the lease beyond June 1991 but they were willing to sell it at the present market rate which would fetch them anywhere between Rs 10 to 12 crore for this building, whose total land area is over 4,000 square metres. The Germans are willing to increase the rent proportionately but obviously don't seem to be in a mood to cough up such an astronomical sum. The Germans' argument is that as per international convention, all properties, lease and deeds of the annexed country automatically get transferred of the unified country.

But the Scindias have thrown Indian law at their faces, which says that tenancy lease can't be transferred. The Germans have tried to use their diplomatic clout but the Scindias have a political prowess to match.

There is another interesting angle to the situation. Though Vijaya Raje Scindia doesn't see eye to eye with her son Madhav Rao, who was a minister in Rajiv Gandhi's cabinet, Madhav Rao had indirectly requested his mother to gift this building to his daughter Chitrangada, who got married to Dr Karan Singh's son Vikramaditya, a couple of years ago. Sources claim that some kind of understanding was arrived at.

Incidentally, Karan Singh is a neighbour to this disputed chancery and the local real estate agents are convinced that now this property belongs to the former ruler of Jammu and Kashmir.

These agents also claim that Scindias and Karan Singh want to build multi-storey flats on this land after demolishing the present structure; and many contractors have visited and taken the measurements for the purpose. But the Germans are adamant over the possession. Their flag still flutters at the rooftop. The building is still manned by the former East German security personnel.

Dream-Houses... Made of Waste

I have been attending diplomatic parties for many years now. It was great tune to begin with, but soon the monotony caught on. The same luces, the same his and byes. In one spring cleaning, I realised I had collected about a dozen visiting cards of the same person and about five each of another, establishing the futility of contact making and that too through cards exchanging. But it's not always the same. There are mighty interesting moments too!

I stumbled upon a person who was here to collect all kinds of Indian wastes and convert them into building material aggregates. Rupees 80,000 for a house of 1,000 square feet, meaning Rs 80 per square foot against the market rate of Rs 600 per square foot. Phew! Some claim that. His company Global Development Concepts has done it in South Africa and Indonesia. They have now come from the outskirts of Philadelphia to sell the concept to Indians who have an incorrigible habit of spreading the liner and insatiable desire to own a house. Every morning dozens of dream-sellers peddle their blueprints through newspapers in the form of residency floors, farmhouses, exotic villas and luxury cottages. But most of them are beyond the affordable limits of most of Indians. Finally, it is the same real estate circuit which keeps on revolving their money.

First, I didn't believe this pony-tailed tall and handsome Oriya, Satya Ranjan Patnaik, with an American accent, who after graduating from JNU went to the US for field research and got settled there. Today he claims to burn all hazardous, toxic and medical wastes, tyres, asbestos at 25,000 degree fahrenheit (five times hotter than the surface of the sun) in a shipping container so that there is no exposure to the personnel, no toxic gas emissions to the atmosphere and no landfill requirements. It not only recovers total fuel value of wastes but gives salable metal and solid residues which can he used to make bricks, counter-tops, bathroom fixlures, floor tiles, patio stones, insulations, mineral wool, road building aggregates, abrasive material, grinding media or shot blast, is the low cost housing copywriters of Housing and Urban Development Corporation (HUDCO) listening?

After listening to all this hi-tech sale talk, I asked him if every thing was so hunky dory what was he waiting for. Bureaucratic clearance and political patronage, of course. Because if his plans come true, he will pack off most of the Indian builders from the business. Also because even Delhi Development Authority (DDA) offers a 1,000 square feet house for no less than Rs 10 lakh and that too in a remote El Dorado such as Dwarka near Pappan Kalan. Out of this, only Rs. 4 lakh in the land cost and that too on a lease basis while Rs 6 lakh are earmarked for construction while our academic-lurned-global corporate vice-president is giving for Rs 80,000.

I don't know whether Indian companies would let Patnaik succeed. But it was an interesting encounter in an otherwise sozzled up congregation full of chartered accountants looking for diplomatic accounts, tennis coaches who train diplomats, children, award giving organisers office bearers hunting for their next victims, cultural impresarios eager to offer a return ticket to Honolulu to any willing damsel in desperation, real estate commission agents collecting the cards of those in need of new houses and interior decorators with their designer business cards.

What do diplomats think about this assortment of Indians in the diplomatic parties?

An ambassador from a Balkan state was more than candid. Said he: "I feel Delhi is a hell of a big market place full of agents and middlemen. Every body is a big name–dropper. Earlier they used to stop at ministers and secretaries, bin ever since their next door neighbour IKG has become the Prime Minister, they use his name as their identity cards. Every host is liberal in sending out invitations because he has to fill the place. Still there is an unending stream of requests asking for invitations. You call one and he will never be unaccompanied. They are more than eager to get themselves photographed and next morning they will start asking for a copy of their picture on the house."

I remember the time when a newly arrived young Spanish diplomat friend of mine mentioned that as many as 11 requests had come to be invited to the Spanish National Day party. The only community which is conspicuous by its absence is our media brethren. Barring a few regular veterans who are invited and make it a point to attend but of late even they seem to have retired or the press corps are generally avoiding these get-togethers. Mainly because most of the time, they are generally held at the peak working hours and secondly there is nothing to write back home about by way of hard news. Even most of the fellow ambassadors just show up and leave quietly to leave the host with the excess baggage.

A 7 p.m. show started it 7.40, because VIP guests including Montek Singh Ahluwalia and Joginder Singh were being fed tea and cakes yonder, while the poor unsuspecting journalists and Shabana Azmi sat and fulminated in the auditorium. Tsk, tsk.

Mercifully the speech-making was brief. Shabby looks absolutely glam and svelte, bobcut with feathery wisps across her forehead. Javed *iniyan* has lost some weight too; all to the good, considering his gorgeous wife.

Yemen's national day celebrations at Taj Palace was the first diplomatic party which I attended after the Pokhran neuclear tests while circulating among the Indian and foreign diplomats I could feel the great impact which the Vajpayee government bravado had created on South Block and foreign envoys based in New Delhi. I could understand the restraint but still loud condemnation on the part of the diplomatic community here but I was quite amused at the reactions of our own men in MEA. The sum total of their reactions is as follows.

Vajpayee government chose a wrong time for this display of its nuclear prowess. It should have first consulted its position at home and then abroad before venturing out in such a dramatic manner. The head-on collision part undertaken by George Fernandes known for its pro-Tibet views was not surprising but he is neither taken seriously here not there. There are conjectures that his statements were a precurser to the five blasts in Rajasthan desert but even he might have been surprised. Having blasted the Indian shakiness over its nuclear policy it should have behaved as a nuclear power. But on the contrary the government started speaking in more voices than one where the left hand didn't know what the right hand was up to. At one hand was the political adviser to the PM – Promod Mahajan and on the other was the locally brewed Madan Lal Khurana who behaved as if he was contesting a municipal election against Pakistan.

Amidst these deafening thunders was the shocking silence of the Prime Minister who was not even behaving as first among equals. Like him Gujral also led a multiparty coalition and his partners also aired their views, at variance with him but only behind closed doors. None of them overstepped his brief and spoke publicly causing embarrassing to the leader as well as the nation. It must be seen to know how much hard work South Block does to befriend and retain the Gulf countries in that mould. Despite these over zealous statements various joint secretaries handling Muslim and other countries did a wonderful job in containing their resentment barring Saudi Arabia no one really criticised India, meaning it was a favourable silence. I also met a couple of education planners namely from National Council for

Educational Research and Training (NCERT) who were apprehensive of the influence of Hindutva on the school curriculum after the advent of Murli Manohar Joshi as the HRD minister. He has already issued orders to include Ayurveda in the school textbooks though BJP has tried to rewrite the Mughal India history both in Delhi and Lucknow but these incorrigble reformists never say die. The educationist are in perpetual fear of the education system being rewritten.

Yemenis are great hosts and that is why they are able to attract the best of diplomatic fraternity at their annual affair. The Yemeni ambassador whom I met personally quite some time ago is gentle, soft and very friendly. I am sure it reflects on Indo-Yemen relationship too. Another notable guest was the information resource officer of the American centre William Richardson who heads all the American libraries in India. He was there courtesy his beautiful Yemeni-Somali wife. The lighter side of the heavy evening was the great buffet which had an unending queue of eager palates to the tittilating courses.

Pandemonium broke out at the Siri Fort auditorium when the stage gave way on being stormed by hundreds of Indian and foreign youths yesterday evening during the performance of Swedish rock concert 'Sky High' organised in collaboration with the ICCR.

It all began when one of the five-piece orchestra men asked the crowd to join them on the stage. The wooden floor of the stage is just not meant for this kind of euphoria.

The plainclothes securitymen's attempts to bring order did not meet with success as the young enthusiasts swarmed the wooden stage creating total confusion. The hall was packed to its full capacity, including scores of foreign diplomats.

In full view, they whisked away some Indian youths to the side greenroom for a thorough thrashing. With the co-organisers Indian Council for Cultural Relations (ICCR) deciding not to interfere, the situation was saved from turning into a melee when a senior Swede diplomat rushed to save the youths.

The incident left many questions unanswered. Whose idea was it to organise a rock concert at the Siri Fort auditorium? Why was no responsible ICCR functionary present there to anticipate and save the situation? And why only Indian youth were picked up for exemplery punishment?

Index

K

L

N

O

P

Q

R

S